The Art of
Woodcarving

BOOKS IN THE CREATIVE HANDCRAFTS SERIES:

JACK J. COLLETTI is a master draftsman and craftsman. His sculptural works are mainly in private collections. He has taught architectural design and construction at Thomas Edison Vocational and Technical High School in Jamaica, New York, and has given in-service courses in woodcarving for the Board of Education, City of New York.

He comes from a long line of sculptors, woodcarvers, and cabinet makers. With this background and interest in following the family forte, it is only natural that the instruction in *The Art of Woodcarving* follows the traditional practice.

The Art of Woodcarving

JACK J. COLLETTI

A SPECTRUM BOOK

PRENTICE-HALL, INC., *Englewood Cliffs, N.J. 07632*

Library of Congress Cataloging in Publication Data

COLLETTI, JACK J (date)
   The art of woodcarving.

   (The Creative handcrafts series)   (A Spectrum Book)
   Bibliography: p.
   Includes index.
   1. Wood-carving. I. Title.
TT199.7.C64   736'.4   76-56442
ISBN 0-13-049247-7
ISBN 0-13-049239-6 pbk.

©1977 by Prentice-Hall, Inc.
Englewood Cliffs, New Jersey 07632

A SPECTRUM BOOK

10 9 8 7

Printed in the United States of America

PRENTICE-HALL INTERNATIONAL, INC., *London*
PRENTICE-HALL of AUSTRALIA PTY. LIMITED, *Sydney*
PRENTICE-HALL of CANADA, LTD., *Toronto*
PRENTICE-HALL of INDIA PRIVATE LIMITED, *New Delhi*
PRENTICE-HALL of JAPAN, INC., *Tokyo*
PRENTICE-HALL of SOUTHEAST ASIA PTE. LTD., *Singapore*
WHITEHALL BOOKS LIMITED,*Wellington, New Zealand*

Contents

Foreword

The 10-year-old whittling a design on a board with his penknife, the rustic carving a magical chain link from a pine branch, the woodcarver completing a floral design in a wardrobe door, and the sculptor transforming the huge wood block into a lifelike figure—these people are all driven by the same urge—to cut away the confining surfaces of a piece of wood and reveal underneath the image born in the mind's eye.

As a master craftsman artist and a veteran teacher, Jack Colletti charts the path between the conception of the image and its final liberation from its surrounding bonds of wood, instructing the reader not only "how to" but "why" and imparting his obvious love and reverence for both the wood and the tools used to shape it.

Jack Drutman

Preface

Anyone can carve! *The Art of Woodcarving* has been written with this thought in mind. It is intended for anyone who wishes to take up a worthwhile endeavor; it is not only for people who want a creative outlet to fill their leisure time but also for those who want to learn the techniques and go on to more serious carving.

The basics are easy to learn. Their application, as described in detail in the carefully selected examples, will make possible the proper use of the tools in any type of wood sculpture. Each example is reinforced by similar additional material that can be adapted to many decorative applications.

The form or structure of each type of carving is presented with the essential characteristics, and although they are arranged in sequence to prepare for the following lessons, each type of carving is complete in itself. Throughout the various lessons the student is guided in using *conventional,* or simplified forms of, designs and adapting them to his needs, and is encouraged to interpret in his own way what he perceives.

At the completion of the exercises in relief carving he should be well prepared for carving in the round if he so desires. Since carving in the round is not unlike carving in relief, he will soon grasp the methods of procedure involved.

Acknowledgments

Grateful acknowledgment is given to Marion Grant for her generous assistance in typing the manuscript; to Jack Drutman for reviewing the manuscript and making helpful suggestions; to Thomas Donzelli for his invaluable help in the preparation of the designs; to the eminent artist Archie Jefferson for his excellent original designs of the zodiac; to Phillip Bleiwas for the superb photography; to Edward Katz and Saul Rosenblum for their technical advice; to my son, Paul, for his many enthusiastic ideas in the organization of material; and to Mary Allen for her excellent copyediting.

Special appreciation is given to my wife for her patience and encouragement.

An Overview

Woodcarving has taken its place in history as one of the oldest of the art forms. It probably began when primitive man fashioned his first crude tools. Archaeologists have estimated that the Stone Age—the first known period of prehistoric culture— began 2 million years ago, lasting to about 6000 B.C. Artifacts dating back more than 1.5 million years indicate that during those hundreds of thousands of years, rough, sharp stones and, later, sharper flint stones served as man's tools. Aside from using these tools to dismember the animals he caught, he learned to use them to cut, gouge, and shape wood for his needs, utilitarian as well as aesthetic. Although it is hard to imagine how any kind of carving could be done with such crude implements, these marked the first steps in the art of decoration and the birth of mental ability that were to mature and spread throughout the world.

The tools necessary for good workmanship were born with the Iron Age, which dates to about 1000 B.C., when man learned to extract metal from ore. Artisans, no longer restrained by the limitations of their crude tools, were able to express themselves more freely. Wood and alabaster carvings, such as the Egyptian carvings on the surface of gems, were indicative of the evolution of fine, sharp tools. The exquisite carvings on arches, doors, and ceilings of the 13th-14th century Spanish Alhambra could never have been executed with the tools of the Stone Age. The spiritual force that flows from these carvings was made possible by the quality of the tools.

It was a slow transition from one period to another, but throughout the world, woodcarving was becoming a major art form. By 1400 the number of artists and sculptors was increasing, many of whom left us colorful examples of woodcarving. During this period Donatello carved a statue of David in wood, decorated the interiors and exteriors of churches, and became a major influence on Italian sculpture.

By 1500, practically every church had been decorated with religious statues and crucifixes. Cornices, capitals of architectual columns, and pediments were embellished with carvings. Michelangelo's first sculptures were done in wood. His excellent crucifix of wood, carved in about 1490 for a monastery in Italy, still graces the altar. One of the best woodcarvers of all times was Grenling Gibbons, an Englishman who not only specialized in floral designs but excelled in human figures and church decorations.

In every country and corner of the world, woodcarving was thriving. It spread from one country to another. The Greeks learned from the Egyptians, the Etruscans from the Greeks, the Romans from the Etruscans and Greeks, the English from the Germans, the Germans from the Italians and French.

In 17th century America, the first woodcarvers were carpenters, whose carvings were limited to simple line designs. In the 18th century the availability of design books inspired cabinet makers and aroused their latent capabilities; their simple folk art soon evolved to a form of classical art. In the 19th century, sculptors migrated to America, bringing with them the traditional methods of specialized work that fostered the growth of sculpture in America.

With the advent of 20th-century furniture making, woodcarvers found themselves in great demand and were assured of

3

An Overview

steady employment, which many artisans preferred to isolated carving jobs done on a commission basis. For a time, the growth of the plastics industry—with its cheap reproductions of furniture decorations, wall plaques, statuettes, and so on—stunted the growth of woodcarving. In spite of this, the recent renaissance of interest in and attention to the folk arts ensures that woodcarving will survive and flourish as it has done throughout the ages. The striking character of wood and its creative possibilities will continue to enthrall art lovers throughout the world.

Since wood is easy to carve, woodcarving can provide you, no matter what your level of expertise, with a new and limitless means of creative self-expression. By handling the same basic tools as your ancestors did you will be rewarded in many ways. Your forefathers have left you a wealth of examples, which you can re-create and build upon.

This book is offered as a guide and a catalytic agent to help you react, with your mind and your spirit, to the visual richness that surrounds you. I hope that it will also be a stimulus for you to make your environment a better one in which to live.

2 General Information

Any wood can be carved! I wouldn't recommend that you try hardwoods like lignum vitae, ebony, or live oak as a beginner, but you will be able to handle any kind of wood once you have learned about the nature of the different types of wood and about the different tools involved, how to use them, and how to care for them.

THE NATURE OF WOOD

There are many qualities that we must consider in choosing which wood we want to use for a particular project. Obviously, weight and hardness have a lot to do with the amount of force that will be necessary for the carving itself. Likewise, the penetration of finishing chemicals, such as varnish and oils, depends upon the type of wood. **Grain*** affects both the look of the finished product and the ease or difficulty with which the wood can be worked. Another important factor is the tendency of some woods to split **(check)** when they are being gouged or cut. Finally, the craftsman must consider the ultimate object and its use—it wouldn't be practical to use an overporous wood to make a vase meant to hold liquid, or a wood that bleaches for an outside decorative piece.

The hardness or softness of a wood cannot always be expressed as such by its botanical classification. Botanically, hardwoods are those trees that shed their leaves in winter. The conifers, evergreens that keep their needle leaves throughout the year, are the softwoods. According to the comparative figures worked out from the fiber stress, the actual characteristics for hardness show that some of the botanically classified hardwoods are soft, while some of the soft are actually hard or semi-hard. For example, willow, chestnut, alder, aspen, basswood, and poplar—botanically classified as hardwoods—are actually soft, while fir, jackpine, and tamarack, classed as softwoods, are hard or semi-hard.

The characteristics of each particular tree are too numerous to allow a short and accurate description of its workability. In fact, in carving on wood from different sections of the same tree, one can never be sure that they will be alike in ease or difficulty of carving.

Again, any wood can be carved, regardless of its classification, but we must take into consideration many factors before we make our choice. Because this is a book for those just beginning to learn about woodcarving, it is only logical to introduce first those woods which carve more easily than others. The list that follows presents some of these:

Basswood. Soft and very easy to carve. Creamy color. **Close grain.** Glues well.

Beech. Even-textured. Close grain. Tendency to split (check). Slightly harder to work than basswood. White, reddish-brown tinge.

Butternut. Easy carving. Light brown. Moderate grain. Usually carved by hand only.

---

*Words that are boldfaced within the text are defined in the section entitled "The Terminology of Woodcarving," which follows.

Holly. Very close grain. Good for detailing. Hard to glue. Carves well. White color.

Linden. Even grain. Excellent workability. Light cream color.

Mahogany. Medium soft. Reddish brown. Outstanding grain. *Honduras*—best to carve.

Pine. Soft, easily carved with sharp tool. Creamy white to light brown. Close, even grain. Types include *northern, western, ponderosa, sugar.*

Poplar. Close grain. Good workability. Glues well. Carves easily. Yellow to brownish-yellow.

Redwood. Good texture, close grain. Deep reddish-brown. Good for outdoors.

Sycamore. Very close grain. Easy to carve. Reddish to peach-brown. Tendency to split.

Walnut. Chocolate brown. Good workability. Varying grains. Excellent appearance. Good for serious carving.

THE TERMINOLOGY OF WOODCARVING

Through the rest of this book, you will be encountering the vocabulary of woodcarving, terms that may be totally unfamiliar (if you have never carved wood before) or with which you may be familiar but in a vague way. The following list, from the simplest to the most complex terms, has been prepared to help you *fully* understand what you will be doing.

Arkansas stone. A natural, oilstone for sharpening and honing carving tools, hard and fine-grained

Band saw. An electric table saw whose blade is a continuous band, this commercial machine permits the cutting of wood up to 6″ thick

Bent gouge. A gouge with a scoop-shaped blade, bent to accommodate hard-to-reach spots

Bevel. The slant that one surface makes with another; the cutting edge of a gouge or chisel

Bevel ground. A bevel or slant produced on a gouge by grinding

Boasting. Preliminary rough shaping of an object to be carved

Burr. The fuzzy or rough edge left on a tool that has been sharpened

Carpenter's chisel. A flat chisel beveled on one side of the blade at the cutting edge

Carver's chisel. See **firmer**

Carving in the round. That type of carving that produces a free-standing object; an object that has been carved in all directions

Chase. A narrow groove made with a veiner; to ornament a carving with long, narrow furrows

Chase carving. Cutting a design in wood with a veiner

Checking. Splitting of wood

Chisel. A tool with a cutting edge that is driven forward to cut, shape, or chip wood

Close grain. Wood fibers that are tightly spaced

Concave. The interior of a carved surface

Convex. The exterior of a carved surface

Coping saw. A small, fine hand saw whose narrow blade is held in a deep frame that permits the cutting of shaped objects

Cross-grain. Wood fibers that run crosswise to the direction of the grain in wood (see **grain**)

Diagonally cross-grain. Wood fibers that run at an angle to the direction of the grain in wood

Eye-tool. A small, quick gouge whose blade has a semicircular curve

Firmer. A flat chisel beveled on each side of the square cutting edge, used to smooth out gouge cuts

Flat gouge. A type of gouge with a slightly curved edge

Fluter. A gouge whose sides extend beyond a semicircle used for carving fluted areas

Garnet. A superior type of sandpaper made from *silicates* (brittle, glossy minerals)

Gouge. A chisel with a curved blade used to cut grooves or holes in wood; to scoop a hollow in wood

Grain. Refers to the direction in which the wood fibers go; affects surface appearance and workability

Grind. To rough-bevel a tool with a grinding wheel

Ground. The bottom or base of a design in relief

Ground in.   To make a cut with a firmer at an angle toward and up to the bottom of a set-in cut

Grounding.   The removal of waste wood pieces made by the gouge after the **setting-in** process

High-relief.   A design that is raised from its background by half or more than half its full natural depth.

Honing.   The fine sharpening of a tool against a hard, fine-grained stone (see **Arkansas stone**)

India stone.   An oilstone made of aluminum oxide; used to sharpen carving tools

Jigsaw.   An electric saw with a blade that operates up and down (called *reciprocating*) in cutting through a curved design

Laminating.   A method of woodcarving in which the design is cut out of one piece of wood and glued to a background

Low-relief.   Also called *bas-relief;* a design raised very slightly above its ground

Modeling.   Curving or shaping to final contours

Oilstone.   A whetstone treated with oil (see **Arkansas stone, India stone**)

Parallel to grain.   Wood fibers that run along with the direction of the grain

Parting tool.   See **V tool**

Pierced carving.   A carving that has been penetrated in parts, leaving no background

Quick gouge.   Also called *scroll gouge;* a gouge whose sides form a semicircle

Rasp.   A toothed abrasive tool shaped like a file, used to rough-shape an object

Relief.   The projection of a figure from a background

Relief carving.   A carving in which the design is raised from its background, so that it stands wholly or partly free (see **low relief, high relief**)

Riffler.   A file-like, abrasive scraping tool or **rasp** that comes in many shapes to fit curved surfaces and hard-to-get-at spots, used to smooth out rough shaping

Rounding.   Shaping the square corners of a piece of wood to round surfaces

Scraper.   A thin rectangular steel plate used to smooth surfaces and remove unwanted surface designs

Scroll.   An ornament with a spiral curve

Setting-In.   The process of cutting along the outline of a design (*set-in*) with a firmer or gouge prior to carving out unwanted wood

Shallow gouge.   A gouge with a slight curve (see **Sweep**)

Shank.   The upper part of the blade of a gouge or chisel

Skew firmer.   A flat chisel (see **firmer**) on each side of the blade at a cutting edge of 45°, used for getting into sharp corners

Slips.   Narrow strips of sharpening stones shaped to fit the contour of carving tools, used in whetting and honing

Straight gouge.   A gouge whose shank and blade are straight

Stropping.   The final stage in sharpening tools, drawing or rubbing the cutting edge of the tool on a thick piece of leather to remove a **burr** and produce a razor-sharp edge.

Sweep.   The curve of the cutting edge of a tool; a smooth sweeping motion made with a tool in cutting wood

Sweep stroke.   Also called *sweep cut,* a deliberate, continuous stroke in shaping a member, or element, of a design, usually with undulating (wavy) surfaces

Undercutting.   Cutting away at an inward angle along the sides of a figure

Undulating.   Wavelike, up and down in a smooth sweep

Veiner.   A small **fluter,** whose high, U-shaped sides extend beyond a semicircle; used for shaping small grooves or indentations

Volute.   A spiral, scroll-like decoration forming the chief features of the Ionic and Corinthian capitals in Greek architecture

V tool.   A gouge shaped like a V, useful in shaping, setting-in an outline, undercutting, and cleaning the sides of upright projections and parting areas between designs.

Waste.   Unwanted material around or within a design in relief, usually to the depth of the ground

Whetting.   Sharpening a tool by rubbing on an **oilstone** or grinding

Zigzag.   A series of short, sharp cuts produced by *walking* (swaying) the chisel in alternate advancing steps; used to produce a textured appearance in desired areas.

3 Tools and Equipment

In order to start off right in carving, it is necessary to have the proper tools and equipment. At the outset, only those tools required for the projects in this book should be purchased. Later, when you have decided on the kind of work you intend to do, you can buy additional tools to suit the conditions of your designs.

When you buy professional carving tools you will notice a slight difference in the sizes given, since some companies give the sizes in millimeters (there are 26 millimeters to the inch). This should not pose any problem, because 1/16 of an inch one way or the other will make no difference.

Chisels and **gouges,** which we will discuss in greater detail later in this chapter, are the main tools of the woodcarver (see Fig. 1). It is best to select chisels and gouges that have octagonal handles made of a dense hardwood—the shape will provide the best control and they will not split when they are struck with a

Tools and
Equipment

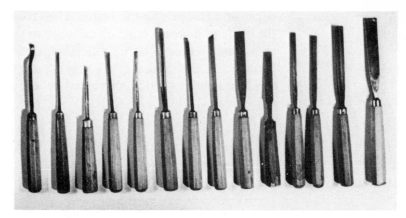

Fig. 1

mallet. These tools usually come rough-ground and must be sharpened before they are used. But it would probably help, for the first time, to order them honed ready for use. This will give you a good idea of what they should look like when they are properly prepared. (We will discuss sharpening later on.)

The angle to which chisels and gouges are usually ground is between 12 and 15°. At this angle they are suitable for most types of work on soft or medium hardwoods, and for the projects we will be doing.

To keep your chisels and gouges sharp, you must have an **India oilstone,** a hard **Arkansas oilstone,** an *India gouge slip,* four *Arkansas slips,* a can of *pike oil,* and a *leather strop* (see Fig. 2). The flat India oilstone is used for removing the fine

Fig. 2

edges and sharpening the blade. The Arkansas stone sharpens the blade to a keener edge. In addition to the sharpening stones, slips (small pieces of hard Arkansas material) shaped in various forms to fit the insides of the carving tools are used to remove any **burrs** or fuzzy edges produced by **whetting** and **honing** (see Fig. 3).

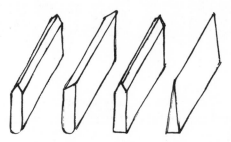

Fig. 3   Carving tool slips

While a *workbench* is an indispensable item for the professional carver, it is expensive, especially if it is bought ready-made with built-in vises. However, it is possible to make one for yourself. It should be high enough for you to be comfortable carving in a standing position. A height of 36″ to 38″ will prove favorable for most people of average height. It should also be strong enough, obviously, to support your work. A good workbench that can be made from ordinary lumber is shown in Fig. 4. If you can afford a *vise,* it can be added to the bench to complete your project. In any event, you will be shown how to anchor your work as you perform the individual projects.

Finally, for the time being, the remaining things you will need are a *whisk broom,* a *carver's mallet* (14 oz), a **rasp**, a **scraper**, and three different-shaped **rifflers** (as shown in Fig. 5).

You will use a whisk broom to clear away the chips from your work and to rub on and into your finished carving, for a fine sheen. The mallet can be used if more than hard pressure is required when you are carving a hardwood; the rasp is for certain rounded parts; the scraper is used to clean off unwanted marks; and the riffler is for hard-to-get-at spots and rough shaping.

Later when we get into relief carving, we will need a few small items, usually found around the house, to make our work easier.

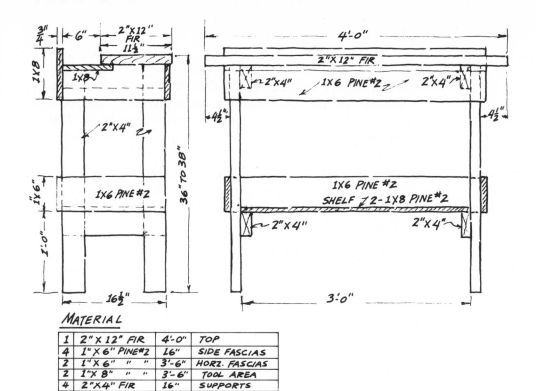

MATERIAL

1	2" X 12" FIR	4'-0"	TOP
4	1" X 6" PINE#2	16"	SIDE FASCIAS
2	1" X 6" " "	3'-6"	HORZ. FASCIAS
2	1" X 8" " "	3'-6"	TOOL AREA
4	2" X 4" FIR	16"	SUPPORTS
4	2" X 4" FIR	3'-0"	LEGS
2	1 X 8 PINE#2	3'-0"	SHELF

Fig. 4   Workbench for woodcarving

Fig. 5

CHISELS AND GOUGES

Carving chisels and gouges, sharp-edged tools used for cutting, chipping, or shaping material, come in many shapes and sizes—probably in the hundreds. Although it would be ideal to have many of these, it wouldn't be practical. They would only clutter the bench top and result in precious time spent searching for the right one. In practice, the average woodcarver has some fifty or sixty tools. Of these no more than ten or twelve are constantly in use. Figure 6 shows the **sweeps** (cutting edges) of the various chisels and gouges.

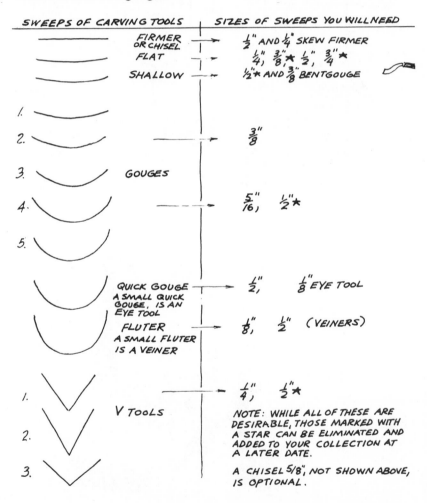

SWEEPS OF CARVING TOOLS | SIZES OF SWEEPS YOU WILL NEED

FIRMER OR CHISEL — $\frac{1}{2}$" AND $\frac{1}{4}$" SKEW FIRMER

FLAT — $\frac{1}{4}$", $\frac{3}{8}$" ★ $\frac{1}{2}$", $\frac{3}{4}$" ★

SHALLOW — $\frac{1}{2}$" ★ AND $\frac{3}{8}$" BENT GOUGE

1.

2. — $\frac{3}{8}$"

3. GOUGES

4. — $\frac{5}{16}$", $\frac{1}{2}$" ★

5.

QUICK GOUGE — $\frac{1}{2}$", $\frac{1}{8}$" EYE TOOL
A SMALL QUICK GOUGE, IS AN EYE TOOL

FLUTER — $\frac{1}{8}$", $\frac{1}{2}$" (VEINERS)
A SMALL FLUTER IS A VEINER

1. — $\frac{1}{4}$", $\frac{1}{2}$" ★

V TOOLS

NOTE: WHILE ALL OF THESE ARE DESIRABLE, THOSE MARKED WITH A STAR CAN BE ELIMINATED AND ADDED TO YOUR COLLECTION AT A LATER DATE.

2.

3. A CHISEL $\frac{5}{8}$", NOT SHOWN ABOVE, IS OPTIONAL.

Fig. 6 Shown in the left-hand column are the sweeps (cutting edges) of carving tools. Each of these is available in 20 sizes from $\frac{1}{16}$" to $1\frac{9}{16}$".

Chisels and gouges operate on the same principle as a plane. The cutting iron of the plane, however, is set for one angle, while the chisel or gouge is controlled by hand for any position or angle. The plane iron is always set with the **bevel** down against the cutting or smoothing surface. The chisel or gouge may be used with any side of its cutting edge in a down position, depending on the kind of cut desired.

When the bevel of a chisel is down on a surface it has a smoothing effect and will not dig into the surface. When the bevel is up, the back flat side will tend to dig into the surface. The **carver's chisel** that has a slight curve (also called a **flat gouge**) will not dig into the wood and is used to smooth out gouge marks produced in **grounding** (removal of the waste).

The carver's chisels are called the **firmer** and **skew firmer.** These are sharpened on both sides.

The firmer is a flat-bladed, double-beveled chisel with a square cutting edge. Because it does not dig into the wood, it is used to smooth out the gouge cuts of a **ground.**

The skew firmer is a type of chisel that has its cutting edge angled. It is used for getting into sharp corners.

In addition to these the carver uses the regular **carpenter's chisel** sharpened to 12 to 15°. This tool is most useful in **setting in** a straight line.

The next important tools are the gouges. These are nothing but chisels with curved cutting edges. Those with only a slight curve are called *flat gouges.* Those with curves of various degrees up to a half-circle are simply *gouges.*

When they approach the half-circle shape, gouges are called **quick** or **scroll gouges.** As they continue beyond the half-circle, the sides extend out without curving. These are the **fluters.** As the name implies, they are used for carving fluted areas. The gouges are used for rounded areas as well as for general roughing-out of a carving and for modeling.

The **V,** or **parting tool,** is the gouge most useful in **modeling,** setting an outline, undercutting, and cleaning the sides of upright projections and parting areas between designs.

The **veiner,** another very useful item in modeling (final shaping) where grooves or small curved indentations occur, is a small fluter with high sides.

Both chisels and gouges can be driven by hand or by mallet; these two methods of carving are illustrated in Figures 7 and 8.

The tools above are the most important of the carving tools. The proper assortment can produce almost any carving.

**Tools and
Equipment**

Fig. 7   Gouging with the mallet

Fig. 8   Gouging by hand
pressure

As you get into serious carving, you may want to add a few
other tools that will make it easier to manipulate in certain hard-
to-get-to spots. For this purpose, the **bent gouges** will be most
useful, especially in tight areas where the grain changes
direction.

The importance of disciplining yourself in caring for your tools is the first factor in woodcarving. The professional woodcarver produces clean-cut, crisp and sharp forms not because he is a professional but mainly because of his sharp tools. He has learned through experience that sharp tools are the chief components of his art.

You will learn this the hard way if you allow your tools to become dull. Your work will not progress properly. The fibers of the wood will be torn instead of cut and produce a roughness on the edges and surface of your work. Remember, carving means cutting away artistically, not tearing and pulling apart by force. You will finally be convinced when you encounter a meeting of wood grain going in opposite directions.

The most obvious ways of caring for your tools involve sharpening and **grinding** them properly. But you must remember to keep the implements for these procedures in good condition. For example, the grinding wheel and sharpening stones need special attention. The grinding surface of your wheel must be kept square. You should occasionally apply an emery stick or diamond wheel dresser to the grinding surface to insure its squareness and to remove any small particles of steel that have become embedded in the grinding of tools. Always slide your tool clear across the wheel surface to insure even wearing of the surface of the wheel.

Oilstones should be treated carefully, too. They should be cleaned and covered after use. This applies to the **slips** as well. Keep them clean and stored away in a cigar box. Occasionally after repeated use the oilstones and slips may be washed with benzine. To keep the stones from falling to the ground and breaking while they are being used, you can anchor and steady them. Remember, to produce professional-quality carvings you must keep *all* your working equipment in top condition.

SHARPENING

As we have mentioned, newly purchased chisels and gouges are only **bevel-ground.** They must be sharpened before they can be used. For this, the operations of **whetting, honing,** and **stropping** are performed.

Whetting

Whetting is done on a flat India oilstone. This process removes the fine edges and sharpens the blade.

Apply a few drops of Pike oil or a light oil mixed with kerosene on the India stone. With the chisel in your right hand, place the bevel on the stone over the oil, so that the full bevel touches the stone. If the bevel is correctly set, the oil should squeeze out away from the cutting edge (if it hasn't already soaked into the stone).

In this position, place the fingers of your left hand over the shank of the chisel—below your right hand—and slide the chisel back and forth along the length of the stone (see Fig. 9). Be

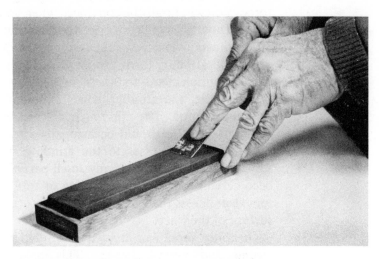

Fig. 9 Whetting a chisel

careful not to change the position of the bevel. After thirty or forty strokes examine the cutting edge and feel for a slight burr or fuzzy edge on the back of the chisel. If none is present, oil the stone and continue the process until one is produced. This slight burr indicates that the edge of the bevel has reached the edge or tip of the back of the chisel—its maximum point of sharpness. The burr is above this point and must be removed. Oil the stone if needed and set the back side of the chisel *almost* flat on the stone; rub it back and forth to remove the burr and produce a short bevel. A carving tool should have two cutting bevels, outside and inside (See Fig. 10).

18

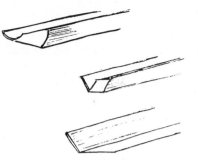

Fig. 10   Carving tools have
two bevels, inside and outside

Later, when you have gotten the knack of holding the full bevel on the stone (usually 12 to 15°), you may flip the chisel from its bevel side to its back—stroke it a few times and flip it back to the bevel side, stroke a few times, and repeat the flipping process until the burr is removed.

Honing

We are now ready to hone the chisel. Honing is done on a hard Arkansas oilstone to sharpen the blade to a keener edge. Oil your Arkansas stone, hold the tool in your left hand and the stone in your right hand (see Fig. 11). Steady your left arm against your body and rub the stone up and down against the

Fig. 11   Honing chisels

bevel of the chisel until all burrs are removed. Use pressure on your downstroke against the cutting edge. Turn the tool to its back and hone the small bevel. Be careful not to round off the corners.

Stropping

Stropping produces a still finer edge. All tools should be stropped before they are used. (And you should keep your strop hung in a readily accessible place, because you must strop frequently to keep your tools sharp.) Finish your sharpening by drawing the tool, with the cutting edge trailing, a few times along a strop of leather (⅛″ x 3″ x 12″) treated with oil or Jeweler's rouge. Any slight burr left over from honing will be removed.

You may now test the blade for its sharpness by drawing the edge lightly across your thumbnail. If it catches—it's sharp! You may also try to cut across the grain on a soft piece of wood. The cut should be clean and sharp.

SHARPENING V OR PARTING TOOL. Both sides of the V tool are sharpened as a chisel. Care must be exercised to sharpen each side equally.

During the whetting, a sharp edge is produced at the meeting of the cutting edges on the beveled sides together with a small projecting point at the apex. These must be removed. Place the sharp edge of the V tool on the India stone and rock it back and forth as in Fig. 12 and round off the sharp edge to conform to the inner angle as in Fig. 13. The sharp tip will also disappear. Then hone the outside bevels and rounded edge. Use a round-edge slip. The inside bevels are honed with a knife-edged Arkansas slip as in Fig. 14. Any remaining stubborn burrs are removed by drawing the edge across the corner of a block of wood.

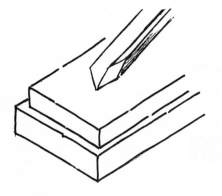

Fig. 12   Removing sharp tip and rounding edge of the V tool—rotate and slide back and forth

Fig. 13   Outside and inside
angles of V tool are equal

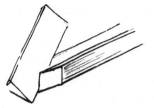

Fig. 14   Use knife slip on
inside edges of V tool

SHARPENING SKEWS OR CORNER CHISELS.   These are also sharpened in the same way as chisels. Hold the cutting edge parallel to the short ends of the India stone. If both sides are equally sharpened, no burrs will be apparent. However, stropping will properly finish off the edge and remove any slight burr still there.

SHARPENING SCRAPERS.   To sharpen a scraper, rub a fine file across the edge of the long thin side until a wire edge is formed. Place in a vise or in a controllable position and with a burnisher (a hardened steel tool) rub along the edge four or five times at a slight angle, applying as much pressure as possible. Increase the angle a bit more and rub as before. Once more, say at an angle of about 15°, repeat the rubbing with the burnisher. The tool should now be ready to use to clean a flat surface or remove irregularities. The scraper is held with two hands, one on each short end. Scrape across the required area with the lowered burnished edge flat on the surface facing the direction of the scraping.

SHARPENING GOUGES.   Whet the outside bevel on the inside of an India gouge slip by rocking it back and forth. The inside bevel is whetted with an India round-edge slip; stroke the oilstone up and down to produce a slight bevel evenly around the curve (sweep).

Follow the honing process explained for chisels (see Fig. 11) but revolve the gouge with the fingers of the left hand while you are stroking the oilstone up and down with your right hand.

Keep the bevel flat on the stone (12 to 15°). From time to time examine the edge of the gouge by holding it vertically and looking down at the edge. A light or white line will be visible if it is properly sharpened.

Bevel the inside edge slightly with a round hard Arkansas slip stone.

Be careful not to round the corners—especially on the deeper sweeps.

After a tool has been sharpened properly, it can be kept sharp by honing and stropping. However, if at any time a tool becomes badly chipped, irregular, or badly blunted, you must grind it to correct the edge.

GRINDING

Grinding is done on a slow-speed emery wheel of medium grit. If the edge of the tool is not square or is deeply chipped, set the tool on the tool rest and feed the cutting edge at right angles to the circumference of the wheel. In this position (with the wheel turning clockwise) the edge of the tool is squared off. You can now grind a new bevel at about 12 to 15° to the wheel surface by sliding the tool across the full width of the emery wheel to insure an even wear of the wheel.

To protect the tool from overheating and losing its temper, dip it in water frequently while you are grinding.

Although a fine cutting edge is produced by grinding, it is not sharp enough for carving. The tool must be sharpened further by whetting, honing, and stropping as already explained.

4 Chase Carving

Chase carving, also called *incising,* is an excellent way to start learning control of your tools. It is not an end in itself but is useful in other forms of carving. The procedure is simply cutting a design in wood with a veiner—a ⅛″ tool. (You will remember that a veiner is a small fluter.)

Preparation and Procedure

Take a piece of pine or basswood about 8″ x 12″. Anchor it to your work area with finishing nails, as shown in Fig. 15.

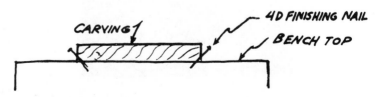

Fig. 15   Anchoring a carving

24

Chase Carving

Directly on the surface, sketch in vertical, horizontal, diagonal, and curved lines (Fig. 16).

Start with the ⅛″ veiner. Hold the shank with your left hand, which controls and guides the tool. Hold the handle with the right hand to push the tool (Fig. 17). Begin with the vertical lines, which are in **cross-grain.**

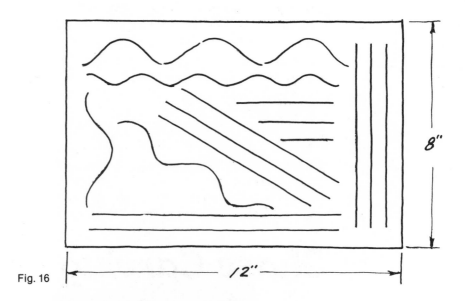

Fig. 16

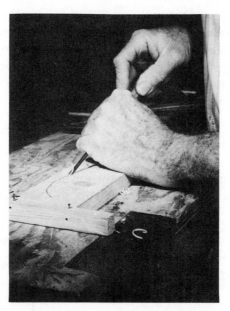

Fig. 17   Carving with the veiner

Set the tool on the low end and slowly but steadily cut along the lines. Your left hand will control the depth. Do not dig too deeply. Try to keep an even cut along the line.

If your veiner is properly sharpened, it will cut cleanly and produce a shine on the cut. Repeat the procedure along the diagonal lines. They too should be sharp and clean.

Now cut on the horizontal lines, which are parallel to the grain. Be careful here—your veiner may have a tendency to dig into the wood. You will need a controlled grip.

Finally, try the curved lines, slowly and steadily, with an even pressure. On the "S" curve, you may run into a little cross-grain. If this occurs, the tool will hesitate slightly and if you continue, the wood will splinter. To avoid this, reverse your cutting (go in the opposite direction).

On the very small curves, place the index and middle fingers of the left hand on the shank with the thumb under. Support the little finger and ring finger on your work. This grip on the tool will make it easier to chase small areas. Try for a complete sweep. You'll soon get the knack. Do not dig in—use only a little pressure with your left hand (see Fig. 18).

Fig. 18

In Fig. 19 are shown various simple **scroll** designs that can easily be adapted for chase carving on flat areas of furniture, picture frames, or any area that could stand a little decoration. Study these carefully and sketch them to a smaller or larger scale. As you draw, try to simplify or add to the design without losing the general feeling of the scroll. A scroll need not follow the forms as shown. It can be adapted to any condition such as those shown below in Fig. 20. The combinations are endless.

Fig. 19

  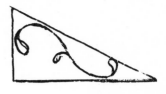

Fig. 20

On scrap wood of pine, basswood, poplar, or other soft-woods, try one or more of these scroll designs with a ⅛″ veiner. See if you can show what you mean with only a few strokes. A few clean-cut sweeping strokes are better than a multitude of meaningless nibbles! Remember the old adage: simplicity is the keynote of quality.

The use of the veiner in these exercises will develop your technique, and this will prove invaluable in the other types of carving you will do.

5 Relief Carving

When you have practiced chase carving enough so that you feel comfortable with the medium, you are ready to start carving in relief. In **relief carving**, the procedures for cutting a design to a given depth are always the same for any given condition.

Choose the wood you are going to work with and transfer your design or draw it directly on the wood. In making a relief carving, you will first have to learn the **setting-in** process; then you will make grounding cuts to remove the extra material; and finally, you will do the **modeling**—the carving or shaping of the wood to its final contours.

SETTING-IN

This process requires you to cut along the outline of the design with gouges having the same shape as the outline. To do this,

28

hold the tool at a right angle to the surface and briskly hit it with a mallet to a depth of ⅛ to ³⁄₁₆ " (see Fig. 21). In making the set-in cuts, be careful not to undercut the design as shown in Fig. 22, especially in small or weak areas. In these cases it would be safer to cut away slightly from the design outline as in Fig. 23.

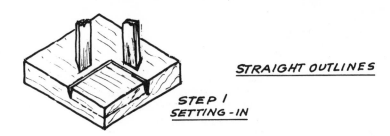

STRAIGHT OUTLINES

STEP 1
SETTING - IN

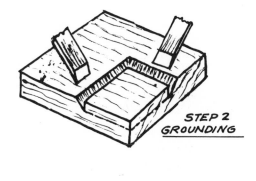

STEP 2
GROUNDING

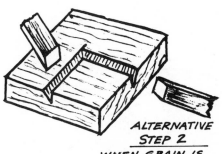

ALTERNATIVE
STEP 2

WHEN GRAIN IS
PARALLEL TO SET-IN,
THE GROUND-IN AREA
MAY BE SLICED.

STEP 3
WASTE REMOVAL
GOUGE CROSS-GRAIN

NOTE: THE FIRMER MAY
ALSO BE USED IN PLACE
OF THE CARPENTER'S
CHISEL SHOWN IN ILLUSTRATION.

Fig. 21a   Steps in starting a
carving in relief

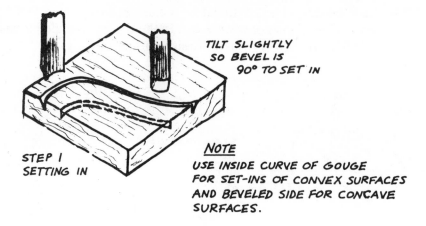

TILT SLIGHTLY
SO BEVEL IS
90° TO SET IN

STEP 1
SETTING IN

<u>NOTE</u>
USE INSIDE CURVE OF GOUGE
FOR SET-INS OF CONVEX SURFACES
AND BEVELED SIDE FOR CONCAVE
SURFACES.

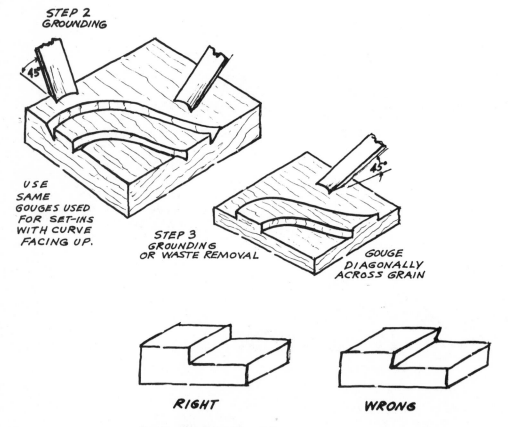

STEP 2
GROUNDING

45

USE
SAME
GOUGES USED
FOR SET-INS
WITH CURVE
FACING UP.

STEP 3
GROUNDING
OR WASTE REMOVAL

45°

GOUGE
DIAGONALLY
ACROSS GRAIN

RIGHT   **WRONG**

Fig. 22   Removing the waste

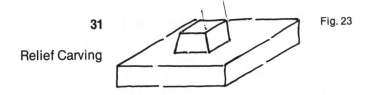

Fig. 23

Be careful in making set-in cuts along the grain. Here you should use less pressure. See Fig. 24 for a detailed diagram of carving in **relief** for straight and curved outlines. (We will have more to say about the grain shortly.)

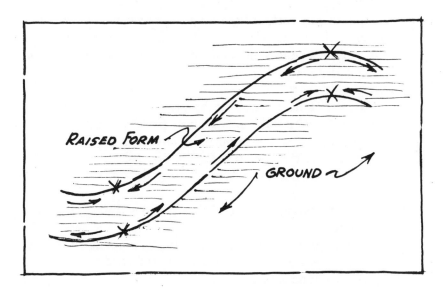

RAISED FORM

GROUND

Fig. 24   Cutting with or against the grain

GROUNDING

When the design is all set in, make a *grounding cut* at an angle of about 45° to meet the set-in cut (see Fig. 21). This is a diagonal cut across the grain of the wood which removes the wood between the set-in and grounding cuts in preparation for removing the unwanted material from the design. (This unwanted material is also referred to as **waste**.) Wasting, or grounding, is accomplished with gouges.

For deeper cuts, repeat the set-in and grounding procedures and remove the waste to the required depth. Then you can make the surface smooth and clean with a flat gouge—a gouge with a slight curve—or a firmer. These are the only tools you should use because they are the only ones that will not dig into the ground surface.

MODELING

In carving of any sort, the graining of the wood must be carefully considered. The X's in Fig. 24 signify approximate spots where the grain changes direction. In these areas, if the direction of the cut is not made carefully, splintering of the wood may occur.

The arrows on the form show the direction in which the gouge cuts diagonally with the grain. In these places it is essential that you clear the ground and smooth the surface in the direction of the arrows to avoid difficulties. Ordinarily, a sharp chisel with a slight curve cutting **diagonally cross-grain** would clear the ground in these areas.

As for the raised surface, following the direction of the arrows is critical, especially if your gouge is not sharp. If the edges of the form are to be **rounded** (using a gouge with bevel up), the direction of the arrows *must* be followed to produce a clean sharp cut and shine.

EXERCISE 1. SETTING IN A DESIGN.

Preparation and Procedure

To set in a design similar to that shown in Fig. 25 to a depth of ⅜", you will need some ¾" x 8" x 10" basswood, poplar, or pine.

Lay out your design as shown in Fig. 24. Anchor your block as explained in the section describing chase carving.

Set in the design. You will need gouges to fit curves and a straight chisel (no curves) for straight cuts. Hit your tool briskly. Depending on your wood, it may be necessary to repeat the setting several times to the required ground.

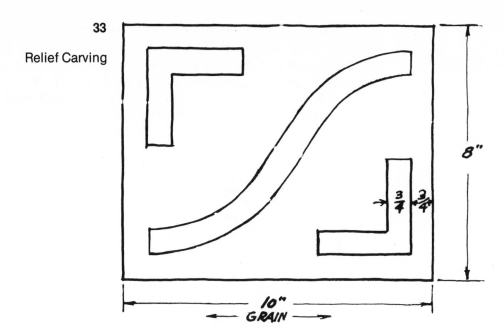

Fig. 25 A design layout

Make a ground-in cut at 45° to meet the first set-in cut.

Remove the waste with one of your gouges.

Repeat this procedure to the required depth. Your carving should look like the sketch in Fig. 26.

Fig. 26 Design after setting-in and grounding

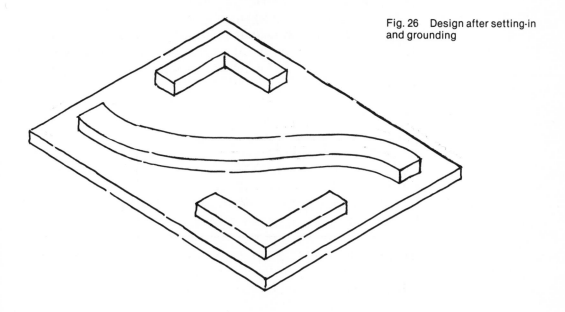

Caution: In setting in the straight outlines always use the flat or back side of the chisel against the design. For setting in curves, the back of the gouge should face *away* from a convex surface and against it on a concave surface (Fig. 27). In this latter case it will be necessary to tilt the gouge so that the beveled edge is at right angles to the side of the outline.

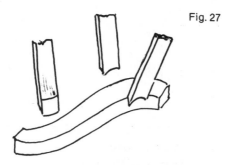

Fig. 27

EXERCISE 2. CARVING ROSETTES

Preparation and Procedure

Divide a piece of pine, basswood, or poplar ¾ʺ × 3ʺ × 9ʺ into three parts, as shown in Fig. 28.

At the center of each square lay out a circle with a diameter of 2½ʺ. You may use a compass or draw free-hand. In square 1, you will carve a four-petal rosette—¼ʺ in relief; in square 2 a five-petal rosette ³⁄₁₆ʺ in relief; in square 3 a six-petal rosette ⅜ʺ in relief.

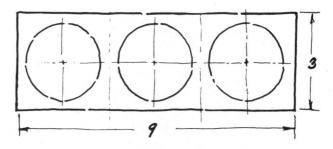

Fig. 28

Divide the circle into four parts.

Lay out the petals—free-hand. Study the rosette in Fig. 29. Observe the layout marks and proceed in like manner.

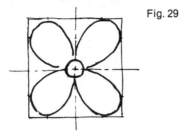

Fig. 29

At the center, draw a ½ ″ circle—free-hand. Your gouges will complete any adjustment as you set in the design.

Set in the small circle (bud) first. One of your small gouges will fit the curve. Make sure you hold it at right angles to the surface. In fact, to avoid any breaking away of the bud, hold your gouge on the line and slant *slightly* away from the bud as shown in Fig. 30. Remember, the set-in should be done in two stages.

Fig. 30

Set in the petals. Your gouges should fit the curve of the petals. If they don't, select those that fit best. Keep track of those used on the first petal and use them in the same way for the others.

Set in the vertical line that separates the first and second squares.

Make your grounding cuts around the petals and remove the waste. Use your gouge diagonally across the grain when possible. Your corner chisel (skew firmer) will come in quite handy in clearing the area where the petals meet.

Repeat the set-in cuts around petals to the required depth and once again remove the waste. Keep the ground level and as clean as possible.

Make the grounding cuts for the set-ins of the center circle (bud). Use the same gouge you used for the set-ins.

Repeat the set-ins to the depth and clean out the waste between cuts as shown in Fig. 31.

The modeling or shaping of the leaves and bud will be done after the other two rosettes are set in and grounded.

 Fig. 31

FIVE-PETAL ROSETTE (⁹⁄₁₆″ IN RELIEF—SQUARE 2)

Divide the circle into five parts. Guess at the adjustment of the compass and by trial-and-error method determine the correct adjustment of the compass to divide the circumference into five parts as shown in Fig. 32.

Draw the five petals as previously explained.

At the center of circle, lay out a ½ ″ circle.

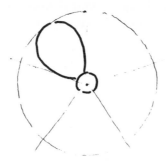 Fig. 32

Repeat the operations of the four-petal rosette. Be careful not to **undercut** (especially the bud). Use the same gouge for setting in and grounding.

Note: Depending on the pressure used for the set-ins, it may be necessary to repeat the operation several times.

SIX-PETAL ROSETTE (⁹⁄₈″ IN RELIEF)

Divide the circle into six parts. Adjust your compass to the radius of the circle (1¼″). It should go six times into the circumference (See Fig. 33).

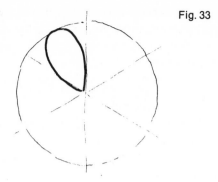

Fig. 33

Lay out the six petals and equalize them as much as possible. Your petals may not look like those drawn by another person. They will be your idea of petals. The sketch in Fig. 34 is only a suggestion of a shape.

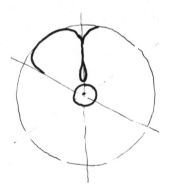

Fig. 34

Draw a ½ " circle at the center.

Set in and ground the design as in the other rosettes.

Set in the vertical division between the rosettes (³⁄₁₆ " deeper).

You are now ready to model or shape out the design of each rosette to its finished contours.

EXERCISE 3. MODELING THE ROSETTES

Preparation and Procedure

In shaping the petals, you can use almost any of the curved gouges. It is all a matter of choice, unless of course you are modeling a specific type, in which case the actual curves (sweeps) and size of the gouge is regulated, more or less, by the design.

For your first rosette use one of the ½" gouges with a medium sweep.

FOUR-PETAL ROSETTE

Hold your gouge as explained and set in, at first, within ⅛" or so from the tip of the petal.

With hand pressure only, and with your left hand controlling the movement, make a deliberate stroke toward the bud. Start with a little pressure and increase gradually as you go deeper into the wood.

As you approach the bud, slow up, decrease the pressure, and stop slightly before the bud. Be careful not to disturb the wood around the bud. The **sweep stroke** of the gouge will influence one of your most important manipulations in producing a sharp clean cut with a shine. In hardwoods, the mallet should hit the gouge in quick successive strokes.

Figure 35 shows the slant of the petals made with the first sweep. You can model the untouched sides with the same gouge by twisting and raising slightly the right side of the cutting edge and sweeping around the curved right portion of the petal as in Fig. 36.

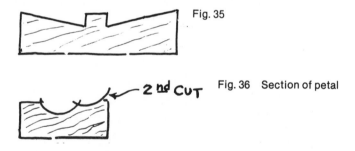

Fig. 35

Fig. 36   Section of petal

Model the left side by twisting and raising the left side of the cutting edge and sweeping around the top left side of the petal and into the original cut.

A word of warning: In modeling around the edges of the petals, be very careful to observe the grain of the wood. Study the grain of the wood in relation to the curve of the petals. You will find that you will be cutting against the grain and with the grain, depending on how the petals are drawn in relation to the grain. If your tools are not too sharp you may produce fuzzy edges and surface. If your tools are sharp, no problem will arise—your cuts will be clean and sharp.

If you are cutting diagonally at first and then curve away to conform to the petal shape and approach a cut parallel to the grain, there will be a tendency for the wood to splinter—even with sharp tools. Stop at this point and cut in the opposite direction, as we discussed earlier. Most of the time you will see just about where this is going to occur, but occasionally it is not apparent until you are actually approaching the spot where a change of direction is required. In Fig. 37 the X's mark the spots where the cutting approaches the splintering possibility.

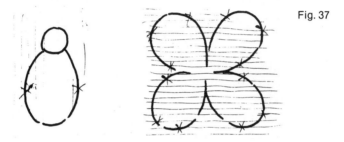

Fig. 37

Fig. 38 shows the direction in which cuts should be made to avoid splintering of wood in a cylindrical design. *Note the critical spots.* Always be careful as you approach them.

Fig. 38

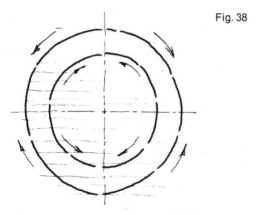

In addition to modeling or cutting circular or curved objects where graining is to be considered, cutting along *with* the grain may create problems as well. This occurs when a seemingly fine grain changes direction to a plane parallel to the grain but slightly below—and continues in the opposite direction.

After you have modeled the other three petals, you can shape the center bud. Here, all that is necessary for the time being is to round off the flat top.

Select a ½" gouge with a small sweep. Hold the shank as usual and set the gouge on the center of the bud. The backside of gouge should be almost horizontal and parallel to the grain so that the figures of your left hand are touching the wood surface.

With the palm of your right hand tap the end of the handle in quick short hammering strokes, while at the same time raising the gouge gradually with each stroke.

As you approach the end of the bud, increase the raising of the gouge until it is almost at right-angles to the side of the bud. Round off the other side in the opposite direction. The depth to which this rounding-off should be done is a matter of taste.

Stand back, study what you have done to the rosette as a whole, and decide whether the bud should stand out or be cut lower.

To make the petals stand out more clearly, set in the bud once more and with the same gouge **ground in** at the set-in cut and remove the waste between (see Fig. 39).

Fig. 39

Finally, with a ¼" V gouge, *carefully* cut two grooves into each petal as shown in Fig. 40. Note how they slant toward the center of the design. As you cut a vein with each petal, start with a little pressure (by hand only) and increase the depth slightly as you approach the grounding-in cut.

Fig. 40

Take the whisk broom and, holding the wisp of straws close to their ends, brush the rosette in a circular motion. This will clear away any small bits of loose chips, as well as producing a fine, even sheen.

FIVE-PETAL ROSETTE

Before any modeling is started, study Fig. 41 and sketch in the upright curled tips of the petals.

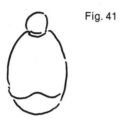

Fig. 41

With your ⅛" veiner, **chase** around the inside edge of each curl.

Repeat the sweep stroke as done for the last rosette. This stroke must start as close as possible to the inside edge of curl (see Fig. 42).

Fig. 42

Set in and ground the curl of petal (³⁄₁₆") as in Fig. 43.

Round off the sharp edge produced by the grounding-in process (see Fig. 44).

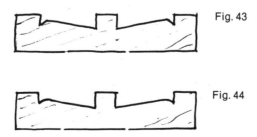

Fig. 43

Fig. 44

Round off the curl in the back and front with a ¼″ flat gouge (slight sweep) as explained for rounding of bud (see Fig. 45).

Fig. 45

Study Fig. 46 and note the shape of the petal; complete side sweeps as shown and as explained for the four-petal rosette. Keep a bit away from the edges.

Fig. 46

When you are satisfied with the modeling, undercut the back of each petal with a flat gouge.

The bud too must now be rounded off. In this case, in using your gouge as before, give this modeling a little more attention. Round it off in all directions. Choose a gouge with a deep sweep. The ends of the bud parallel to the grain will be rounded off with this tool, but the sides will probably not appear as rounded.

To round off the sides of the bud, select a gouge with a small sweep and model with the direction of the grain as shown in Figure 47.

Fig. 47

Round off the bud in all directions as shown in Fig. 48.

When the bud is smoothly rounded, use a small veiner or V tool and chase in the criss-cross design of Fig. 49.

Fig. 48

Fig. 49

With the same veiner, chase in three veins in each petal in the same manner as explained for rosette #1.

Finally, use the whisk broom and rub briskly on the rosette.

SIX-PETAL ROSETTE

This is left entirely to you. Study the six-petal rosette in Exercise 2 carefully and decide how you would like to model it.

If you have diligently followed the instructions for relief carving of the rosettes, you probably have learned that while it takes practice to be able to handle the various gouges, what you soon will have to show for your efforts will make it all worthwhile. To see a form gradually emerge from a blank piece of wood brings a feeling of accomplishment and pride that is hard to match. And you will gain much from the relaxed feeling brought about by working with your hands, oblivious to all but the creation of something that is uniquely yours.

Wood is easy and pleasant to carve, and it becomes easier as the handling of the tools becomes second nature. Modeling of the various forms to create the finished product is what ultimately produces a professional appearance. And each day you learn something new that adds to the joy and rewards of carving.

6 Low-Relief Carving

A combination of chase and **low-relief** carving is adaptable to designs of geometrical forms and scrolls that unite in graceful arrangements. In this form of carving, the design is left flat on the surface of any flat or rounded area. The background is cut back to 1/16″ to 1/8″ and left rough. Low-relief carving is used to decorate furniture (chairs and chests, for example), signs, and plaques. But regardless of the design, the procedure is always the same.

Preparation and Procedure

First draw your design directly on the area to be carved, or trace it on with carbon paper. Chase the outline of your design with a small veiner and remove the background or waste with a gouge. While the gouge marks are usually left in the direction of the design, vertical gouge marks or an entirely smooth surface may be appropriate in some patterns.

Fig. 50 shows a number of simple designs from circular forms. Study them closely and notice how the designs are developed from the basic circle or arc.

Fig. 50

The designs are all drawn free-hand and are merely suggestions for this type of carving. In adapting a design to a given surface, you will find a compass and French curve most useful, but don't underestimate your ability to sketch any of these designs free-hand.

For practice in this area of carving, choose any one of these designs and carve it on a piece of poplar or basswood 4″ × 14″ × ¾″.

Provide a border of ½″ around the design with ⅜″ allowance between the inside of the border and the design. Use a ⅛″ veiner and a ⅜″ gouge. Chase the design and the inside of the border first, then remove the waste. Make your finish gouge marks horizontal. A section of your design is shown in Fig. 51.

Fig. 51

High-Relief Carving

High-relief carving is similar to low-relief, the difference obviously in the depth of the carving. While low-relief carving is limited to a shallow background, high-relief work actually has no limitation.

In addition, the background may be eliminated completely in high-relief carving. Without a background, high-relief carving very closely approaches **carving in the round,** which we will discuss presently. High-relief carving is employed on architectural ornamentation, furniture, wall plaques, frames, etc. It is not free-standing as is a carving or sculpture in the round.

The effectiveness of a relief carving depends on the modeling of the design and not in its depth. A well-modeled low-relief carving can be more effective than one poorly modeled in high relief.

47

48

**High-Relief
Carving**

High-relief carving in architecture employs the use of conventional forms of flowers, branches, leaves, vines, etc., interwoven in an imposing series of scrolls. The best examples are to be found in the capitals of the Ionic, Corinthian, or Composite orders in architecture—these are embellished with such conventional forms joined together in intricate high-relief patterns.

Figure 52 shows a number of individual conventionalized leaves, flowers, and scrolls. Study them carefully and try to sketch them in different positions. Get the feel of drawing a scroll in a continuous curve.

Fig. 52

49

Then study Fig. 53 and observe how the individual shapes of the leaves are used in the scroll designs. These are not as difficult to draw as they appear if you follow the steps shown in the figure. Try a few.

Fig. 53

STEP 1

STEP 2

STEP 3

Figure 54 shows a design suitable for your first try at carving in high relief.

Fig. 54

On a piece of pine, basswood, poplar or any softwood 11″ × 2¾″ × ¾″. Lay out the design according to the dimensions shown. The width of the scroll is ⅜″. Note how you might make use of the concentric circles to help you in the layout. Although these circles have been drawn free-hand, you may prefer to draw them with a compass.

Draw the continuous scroll first—free-hand. Start with the top single curve. Note how it starts at the top of the circle (¼″ from the border) and ends at the bottom of the lower circle. Follow the diagram and complete the scroll. Make your lines very light. Add the curled-up parts as shown. Blacken in your outline.

If you prefer, you might lay out your sketch on paper and trace it on the wood with carbon paper. Anchor your wood as previously explained.

50

Use your ⅛" veiner and chase the outline of the design and the border. Set in the design with the gouges that best fit the curves. Set in the borders with your ½" V tool—do the **cross-grain** borders on ends first. Make two passes, keeping your tool in the normal position. This will give you the slant of the V tool. Ground in with your ½" flat gouge or one with a little more curve. Repeat the setting-in and grounding ½" below the top surface. Remove the waste diagonally *across* the grain. As you approach the ground use your gouge *with* the grain.

Caution: Do not undercut—it is better to slant the gouge away from outline and later make the proper adjustments. Control your gouge as you near the set-ins. Do not start modeling before the entire ground is removed. Observe the direction of the grain on the scroll before modeling.

Plan your modeling beforehand. In this design the curled-up parts are left high at the start of the curls and swoop down. They are rounded off at the start. The rounded parts continue to about the center of each scroll and gradually end in a **concave** cut at the curls. Use your gouge with the concave sweep down in rounding curls and taper off toward the center of the scroll. (Be careful at the transition of **convex** to make a concave cut at each curl.)

Your deepest cut on the scroll should not be closer than 1/16" to ground. You may use your ½" V tool to straighten and clean the sides of the scroll. Don't dig into the ground. Finally, clean up the ground with your gouge cutting **parallel to the grain.**

8 Pierced Carvings

Carvings in which the entire background is removed are adaptable to ornamental designs with branching or interlacing scrolls. (See Figs. 97 and 109 for examples of **pierced carvings**.) The background is removed with a **jigsaw**. While it is possible to cut out the background with gouges, it isn't practical. When the design has been drawn or traced on the wood, holes are drilled in each area requiring a cutout—to start the saw cut. If only a few holes are involved, they can be managed with a **coping saw**. Carvings that require, say, thirty or forty holes should be done by someone who is skilled in this procedure.

In a large panel in which light or ventilation is a factor, a pierced carving may be the answer. Small panels and borders are usually used in the design of period furniture, grills, vents, music stands, etc.

Generally, when a design calls for a bold free-flowing form, the carving is made in high relief. One that is not so pretentious is carved in low relief. Some open-work designs may not require any carving.

Preparation and Procedure

Fig. 55 shows the left half of the next design you will work in your study of carving. Look at it carefully and note the areas to be pierced. In laying out a design that is symmetrical

Fig. 55

about its center, it is customary to draw only one half of it. You can then reproduce the other half by tracing the design of the first half with carbon paper as explained below:

Lay out the left or right half of the design on a sheet of paper wide and long enough for the entire layout below in Fig. 56.

Fold the paper back at the center line (Fig. 57).

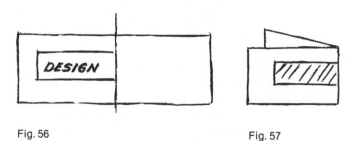

Fig. 56   Fig. 57

Place carbon paper on the back of the folded half, with the *carbon side facing the design.*

Trace the design to obtain the right or left half.

The overall dimensions of the pierced carving for this project are ¾″ × 3″ × 14″. The ⅜″ border is to remain. The areas marked "X" are to be pierced. The outside perimeter should be cut with a jig- or coping saw to save time and eliminate the need for setting in and removing the waste. The material you should use is mahogany or walnut.

When the wood has been pierced, you will center and glue it with a thin glue to a scrap piece of material ¾″ × 5″ × 16″, which you will use as a base. First trace the design on the board through the piercings to spot the placement of the glue. Place a sheet of newspaper on the glued area. Apply another light coat of glue to the newspaper and to the underside of the carving and set the carving on the glued paper. Make sure the glued areas contact each other. Apply pressure, using clamps or some heavy weights placed on the glued wood. Allow to dry according to manufacturer's instructions. Later, when the carving is finished, you can remove it by applying a firmer under the newspaper and gradually separating the carving from the base.

This method of gluing the carving to the base allows you to anchor the base itself to the work bench by tacking it with two four-penny finished nails. In this way the unsupported or weak parts are held firm and prevented from breaking off while you are carving.

In carving this piece, use as many bold deliberate strokes (sweeps) as possible—grain permitting. Rough out the carving before making any attempts to give any finishing touches to the modeling. Take the roughing down to the desired areas. The several parts that overlap the border are to be left high. They may be set in about ¼″ and grounded in. Later the entire border will be lowered ¼″.

Before making any cuts, study the grain—and make sure your gouges are sharp! With sharp tools you should have no difficulty in cutting across-grain.

Set in all the inside outlines. Use the gouges (small and large) that best fit the curves. Use your ½″ parting tool for fast removal of material between tight areas. Start with your ½″ gouge at one of the overlapping leaves and sweep down gradually in the direction of the curve, toward its start. Disregard any part of the design that may be in your sweep.

Remember that few leaves are actually flat in shape. Most of them have various wavy twisting shapes. Although they may be carved with a series of normal cuts, the best way to model or shape them is with a sweep cut. The sweep cut is performed by a combination of movements of the gouge done in one continuous stroke. As the tool is pushed by the right hand, two fingers of the left hand on the **shank** control the direction of the sweep. Leaves with simple curved sides would entail two movements in one stroke. Leaves with undulations (waves) in addition to curved sides call for three movements in one stroke. This third movement is performed by raising or lowering the wrist of the right hand as it pushes the tool. All three movements should be executed in one continuous stroke or pushing of the tool. If you expect to do any serious carving, you should perfect the sweep cut. A little practice on waste wood will reap dividends, for it can be applied to curved surfaces of any carving.

Again repeat the sweep with the other projecting leaf—along the shape of the leaf and down to meet the first sweep. These two gouge cuts should have brought you down about ¼″ toward the center. The cuts should now give you an idea about how the other leaves should be gouged toward the meeting of the first two leaves cut.

Again with your gouge at the overlapping stem of the extreme left leaf, make a sweep gradually down to meet the other cuts. Replace any inside lines you may have removed in rough gouging. Study the design and gouge deeper (about ½″) in the shaded areas and determine which leaves you want in front or back of each other; start gouging each leaf according to the suggested sections shown on each leaf.

Before you shape up the various parts, cut down the border ¼″. Scribe a line along the sides ¼″ from the top surface as a guide. Use a ½″ flat gouge diagonally cross-grain and gradually arrive at the required ground.

Notice how the carving has sprung out.

To shape up your carving use a 1-⅜″ flat gouge, round off the various leaves and ribbon, neatly clean up all corners and intersecting parts with your small skew. Undercut the sides of your vertical leaves to liven up the parts to a more natural form. Use your ½″ flat gouge and cut down and inward with a strong brisk stroke. Finally, use your ⅛″ veiner or small V tool and vein the leaves as they are shown in the figure.

At this stage go on to the central part of the design and ground in the **volute** (spiral) as shown in Fig. 55 by the arrow.

The arrow starts at the highest part of the volute and its direction indicates a gradual downward shape around the volute and down toward the center of the leaf, where it starts coming up gradually to meet the high part of the leaf at the border. Repeat this procedure for the other volute.

Set in and ground the other leaves around the voluted leaf to about ¼ ″ depth. Follow the shape of the leaves and gouge them to produce the given shapes. Repeat the procedure for the leaves of the other volute.

The design is now sufficiently roughed out so you can model each part as indicated by the curved lines.

When you are satisfied with your work, separate the carving with your ½ ″ firmer. Round off all the back edges with your rifflers. Use your whisk broom over the front of your carving, and you are finished.

Fig. 58 shows a few examples suitable for pierced carving as well as for carving in low or high relief. Practice drawing some of these in single line form and you will soon discover how to lay out your own designs.

Fig. 58a

Pierced Carvings

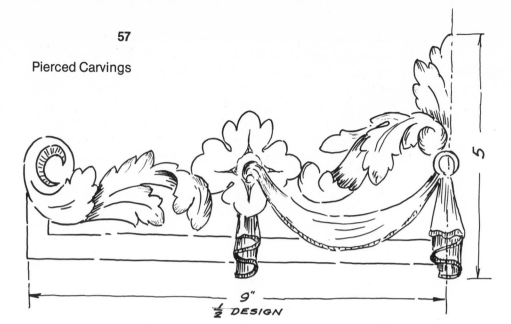

9"
½ DESIGN

Fig. 58b

9 *Laminating Wood*

Your next carving will introduce another method of preparing a subject—the **laminating** method. For this, the design is cut out with a jigsaw or coping saw and is glued to a permanent background. This method not only saves time and work, but is practical in cases in which the required thickness of wood is not available. In addition, the combination of different woods in laminating gives your project a different look, which can be quite effective.

PISCES

To explain the laminating method we will describe a carving of Pisces, a zodiac sign. This design is shown in Fig. 59. The subject is within an 8″ circle, centered on a 10″ square background.

Laminating Wood

The relief is 1⅛″. The material can be pine, basswood, or poplar. You will need one piece ¾″ × 10″ × 10″ and one piece ¾″ × 8 × 8″ square block.

Preparation and Procedure

Draw directly or transfer the outline of the fish on the 8″ × 8″ block. Keep the grain horizontal to the design.

With jig- or coping saw cut out the fish shapes.

On the 10″ × 10″ block lay out an 8″ circle.

Position the fish within the circle and trace the outlines to determine the area on which you will place the glue.

Apply the glue to the traced area and the underside of the fish.

Reset the fish in position and apply pressure (use clamps or a heavy object). Allow the glue to set as per manufacturer's directions.

When the glue has set, the piece is ready to be carved. Tack it to your work area as has been previously explained. Since the overall depth of the relief is 1⅛″, you will be cutting ⅜″ below the surface of the square block within the circle.

Now, before you remove any wood in the circular area, draw in the bubbles of the design and set them in.

With a ⅛″ veiner, chase along the drawn circle. Hereafter, keep within this border while grounding the additional ⅜″. The border should curve in gradually to this depth.

Use a larger veiner or small gouge as you go deeper along the inside of the border. The bubbles are to be left about ³⁄₁₆" above the ground.

Be careful as you remove the waste not to disturb the bubbles. To insure round bubbles, set your gouge partly in your first set-in and the arc of the circle. Follow this same procedure when you are modeling the eyes. Be careful not to undercut!

From here on in, it's up to you. Study the stages of development in Fig. 60; use them as a guide and interpret in your own way what you perceive.

Fig. 60a Stage 1

Fig. 60b Stage 2

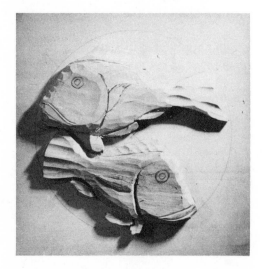

Fig. 60c Stage 3

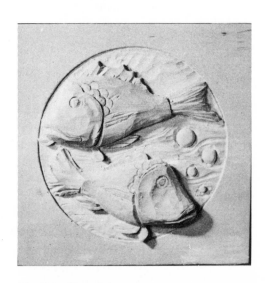

Fig. 60d Stage 4

Laminating Wood

Note: If you prefer to start from scratch instead of using a jigsaw, use a circular block with a ¾ ″ × 8 ″ diameter. Glue it to the base, lay out your design, set in the design, remove the waste, and start modeling.

From the beginning of your first carving lessons in this book to the section on carvings in relief, the various projects presented have been selected as the best means of introducing the methods that would develop the skills in the shortest possible time. Carving the various shapes of the scrolls, leaves, compound curves, and so forth should by now have given you the opportunity to become familiar with the tools and learn to handle them well. However, although the carving of intricate combinations of such designs is useful and applicable in ornamentation, it should not be the pinnacle of your attainment in carving. You should be able to use this knowledge as a stepping stone to more serious carving.

By now you should be well-prepared for carving in the round. This is not unlike carving in relief, so you can look forward to favorable results. You are now ready to give your attention to your interpretation of a subject and not merely to the cutting away of wood. You are free to model or shape a form with a definite purpose in mind—to have it say something by a gesture, a position, or a facial expression. This is the highest attainment of woodcarving. This is what makes carving an art!

10 Carving in the Round

The closest you have come to carving in the round has been in your pierced carving. Had you extended the sides of the scrolls to the back, you would have created a three-dimensional shape—a carving in the round. While all carving is sculpture, the term is more specifically applied to figures or forms that are free-standing and shaped in all directions. Carving in the round is not unlike carving in relief, but positioning the object for proper manipulation may present problems as the sculpture progresses.

Choosing a subject to carve is not as easy as it may appear, especially for a beginner. Your choice should depend on your ability to execute the work. When you have decided what you will carve, you should study the subject in an effort to execute a complete and unified creation. Later, as you acquire facility, ease, and skill in handling your tools your choices will be unlimited.

62

For your first attempt at carving in the round you will have a very familiar subject—a graceful animal with a long bushy tail and strong hind legs for leaping—the squirrel.

SQUIRREL

Figures 61 and 62 show rough sketches of the squirrel in two positions—one in the act of chewing on an acorn and the other in an alert position holding onto his prize. Select one of these for your sculpture. I'm sure you will also end up doing the other one. The procedure is the same for either one. The material used is poplar.

Fig. 61   Squirrel, head down

Fig. 62   Squirrel, head up

Fig. 63 shows a design of the first squirrel as it appears from three views. This will also apply to the other except for the position of the head.

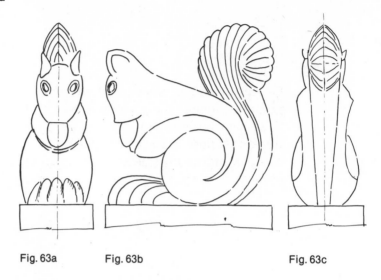

Fig. 63a   Fig. 63b   Fig. 63c

In preparing your sculpture study the methods given below and proceed accordingly.

Preparation and Procedure

METHOD 1 (using 1″ wood pieces glued together for the required
    thickness of 3″)

Draw the design on the wood.

Use a jig- or coping saw to cut out waste in each of the three pieces of 1″ stock.

Glue the pieces together.

Model the squirrel as shown in the stages in Fig. 64.

METHOD 2 (using solid wood 3″ × 6½″ × 10½″)

Draw the design on the wood.

Have someone cut out the waste on a **band saw.** (You may have to go to a specialist because the band saw is a commercial machine not readily available for home use.)

Roughly shape (**boast**) and model the squirrel (Fig. 64).

Carving
in the Round

Fig. 64a   Stage 1 (same for
squirrel, head down)

Fig. 64b   Stage 2

Fig. 64c   Stage 2 (head down)

Carving
in the Round

Fig. 64d   Stage 3

Fig. 64e   Stage 3 (head down)

Draw the design on the wood.

Remove the waste with gouges (Fig. 64). Follow the suggestions given for boasting in Fig. 65.

When you are ready to rough-shape (boast) the squirrel, study the detailed instructions of Fig. 65. Make sure you understand the symbols shown in the legend to indicate the shapes of the various parts. The shapes shown are only suggestions. You may alter any of these as you see fit.

Gouging across the grain should not present any problems. Be careful when you are carving in the direction of the grain. You must boast the entire object before any finishing is attempted.

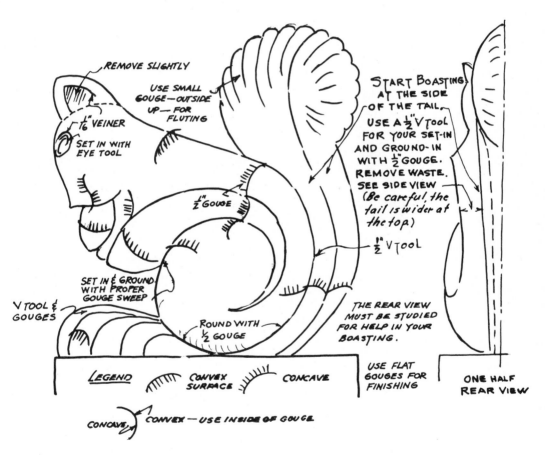

Fig. 65

Set the carving on a ¾ " board and place wood strips snugly against all sides of the carving to anchor it. Tack the wood strips to the board with four penny finishing nails as shown in Fig. 66. In this setup the work may be shifted and tacked or clamped to the bench in any convenient position.

When you have boasted one side of the carving, reset the other side as before and boast in the same manner. Small wedges may be necessary to steady the work when you are working on the second side.

Fig. 66

Most of the finish modeling can be done with the same setup.

The front, rear, and top can best be handled by clamping the work in a vise or by screwing it to a ¾ " board through its bottom with two 1½ No. 10 screws as shown in Fig. 67. This setup can be tacked or clamped to the bench in any desired position.

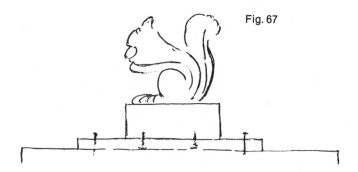

Fig. 67

If you have carefully followed the instructions and completed the assigned projects so far, you should know the capacity of your tools. In the projects that follow—making an owl and an elephant and an eagle—you should have no trouble in carving the simplified forms to produce objects in the round. Each of these present a unique way of preparation that can be used for similar carvings of animals.

OWL

Preparation and Procedure

The material is white pine. The overall dimensions are 10″ × 5¼″ × 4½″. To obtain the 5¼″ thickness (front), glue three pieces of white pine 1¾″ thick together with the grain vertically. Then draw or trace the owl, including the base on which it sits, on each of the three pieces of pine. Cut out the profile of the owl with a coping or jigsaw. Apply glue to each side of the gluing areas and carefully align and clamp them together. Allow about three hours before carving.

Your shaped owl should look like the figure in Stage 1 (Fig. 69).

Roughly outline the shape of the front view of the owl as in Fig. 68 and clamp the base in a vise with the side view up.

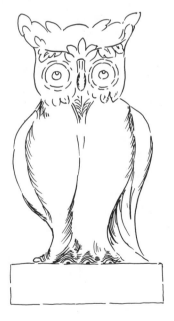

Fig. 68a   Owl, front view

Fig. 68b   Owl, side view

Throughout your boasting of the owl, the base will provide the clamping support so you won't have to move any part of the carving. When you have completed the modeling, smooth the sides of the base with the chisel.

Use a ¾″ gouge and boast the owl to the rough outline of the front view. Repeat the boasting on the opposite side, then turn the owl with the front view up and boast the front as in Stage 2 (Fig. 69).

Outline the head of the owl in the blank area shown and rough-boast it. At this stage you might lay out the eyes so that the rest of the boasting may proceed accordingly.

Stage 3 shows the progress to this point.

Stage 4 shows the completed owl from the front and side views after you have removed the heavy gouge marks and modeled the wings and body shape, the facial features, and the crown feathers. For the intersections of the crown and head, the head and body, the wings and body, use a V tool followed by a ⁵⁄₁₆″ or ½″ gouge to smooth out the transition from one part to another.

Carving
in the Round

Fig. 69a   Stage 1 (side)

Fig. 69b   Stage 2 (front)

Carving
in the Round

Fig. 69c   Stage 2 (side)

Fig. 69d   Stage 3 (side)

Fig. 69e   Stage 4 (front)

Fig. 69f   Stage 4 (side)

In the finished piece, the feathers are shown in the crown and around the eyes. The rest of the owl is finished with gouge marks that represent feathers. You can sand the face of the base section with some **garnet**-grade sandpaper.

Four-legged animals are most easily carved when two halves of the mammal are glued together. The grain of the wood should run vertically, or parallel to the legs. In this manner, each half can be anchored on the bench as shown in Fig. 70 and

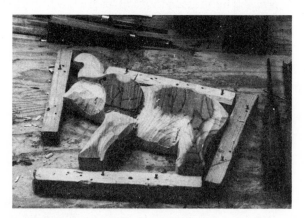

Fig. 70

most of the boasting can be completed before you glue them together. The inside of the legs should not be removed until most of the modeling is finished, because the extra thickness will help support the legs when the piece is clamped in a vise so you can complete the finishing touches.

The elephant shown in Fig. 71 is a good example of carving in sections. Incidently, this method has advantages over using

Fig. 71   Asian elephant

a solid block. Cracks are less likely to occur, anchoring is simplified, and most of the carving can be done in a normal carving position. Also, it is more difficult to find larger solid pieces.

Preparation and Procedure

The overall dimensions of the finished piece are 8⅜ × 8⅜″ × 3½″. The material is poplar with a thickness of 1⅜″, which is available in most lumber yards. Two pieces glued together will be 2¾″. To make up the difference, which occurs only at the high points of the stomach, ½″ material is added (glued) to each side of the elephant's stomach. Follow the various stages shown in Fig. 72 as you work on this project.

Fig. 72a Stage 1

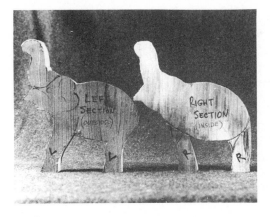

Fig. 72b Stage 2

Carving
in the Round

Fig. 72c   Stage 3

Fig. 72d   Stage 4

Fig. 72e   Stage 5

Fig. 72f   Stage 6

Fig. 72g   Stage 6 (optional
view)

Fig. 72h   Stage 7

On a piece of poplar $9'' \times 9'' \times 1\frac{3}{8}''$, with the grain running vertically, draw or trace the elephant. With a coping or jigsaw cut out the profile. Label this "left section" (outside) and label the legs "L" as shown.

Superimpose the elephant shape on another block of poplar $9'' \times 9'' \times 1\frac{3}{8}''$ and trace the outline. After cutting out the shape, label it "right section" (inside). Label the legs "L" as before.

On the left section remove the right legs (R) and on the right section remove the left legs (L).

Study the photo to determine the position of the right legs as they are shown extended by dashed lines to the body. Note that on the left section the left legs (L) are shown by full lines, while the right legs (R) must be extended to the body.

The left legs of the right section are cut along the dashed line (extended line) of the right legs.

Start with the left section, anchored as shown. Outline the position of the ear and chase it with a small V tool. Set in the outer right part of the ear and ground in to about ⅛" depth. A half-inch to the right of the top part of the ear glue a ½" × 2½" × 2½" piece of poplar centered between the back and the bottom of the stomach. Clamp or hold down with a heavy object.

Repeat this procedure on the right section. Remember, the part marked *right section* (inside) is placed against the bench surface. The head should be facing to the right. Allow about three hours before carving.

Again, start with the left section (anchored) and set in the right side of the ear to a deeper depth (about ¼"). With a ¾" gouge, round off the body starting from the center of the stomach—up toward the back, and from the center of the stomach—and down toward the bottom of the stomach. As you approach the legs use the V tool and extend the legs into the body about 1" or so.

Continue with the ¾" gouge and round off the rear of the elephant in the direction of the grain.

Be careful—if you see a slight splintering, stop and gouge in the opposite direction. Round off the legs.

Studying the photo, outline the curve of the trunk that enters the head, and the curve of the neck and mouth. Use a ¾" gouge and boast the trunk, neck, and mouth areas. Study the ear more carefully and boast with a ⅜" or ½" gouge.

Leave the eyes until last. They will go within the triangular area created in boasting the trunk and neck areas.

Remove the carving and reset the anchoring pieces for the right section. Repeat the operations explained above. Remember, when you round the rear leg, the tail is to remain attached to it. The open space of the leg and tail is gradually made with a ⅜" flat gouge, the leg and tail portion alternately until an opening is created.

If the anchoring piece interferes with the gouging, it can be removed and relocated.

When you are satisfied with the general boasting, the two sections may be glued. However, before gluing, turn over each section to the inside flat areas and set in and ground in the upper parts of the legs where they join the body to a depth of ¼".

The removal of these parts will make it easier to remove the inside thickness of the legs when you are ready to shape the legs. In the meantime, the extra thickness will add supporting strength to the legs.

Glue the sections together. Set the elephant upright on its legs to make sure of proper alignment. Clamp the sections (use clamps or strong cord bound tightly).

When the glue is set, place the carving in a vise with the mouth and trunk in an upright position. Use a V tool for the outline of the outer jaws and again for the inside of the mouth to form the tongue. Use a ½" gouge for the center of the inside of the trunk and mouth. The tongue can be brought out (up) if you use a small flat gouge and cut the lips down lower than the tongue. Do this gradually and each time use a small V tool where the tongue meets the lips, before cutting down on the lips.

While you have the elephant in this position, you may form the curled-up end of the trunk with a small gouge.

Reset the carving in an upright position in a vise with the tail facing you. Use a ½" gouge or fluter and gouge the back of the elephant on both sides of the center line to form a slight ridge for the spine. Do it in several strokes—then gradually blend into the body any other ridges made by the gouge.

Remove the inside extra thickness of the legs and shape out the legs. Use a ½" flat gouge.

Use the rasp and remove all gouge marks. Follow up with the rifflers, then sand with rough garnet paper, and again with a medium grade followed by a fine grade (#000).

To complete the carving, set in the eyes in the triangular area previously mentioned. Use a small V tool for the outline of the eye and a small gouge for the pupil. Round off the pupil with the same gouge, concave side down.

AMERICAN EAGLE

Another popular carving that is prepared by gluing several pieces together is the American eagle. This figure can be used for many other similarly positioned bird carvings. By following the various stages shown in Fig. 74, you can reproduce the piece in any size desired with very little of the tedious work involved in removing waste material.

On ¾″ poplar or white pine, lay out the profile of the front view of the carving. The spread of the wings is 14″, the height is 7″. The grain of the wood should run horizontally. Cut out the shape with a coping or jigsaw. Prepare two pieces of wood 6½″ × 2½″, grain running vertically, on which you will draw the front view of the eagle. Cut out the profile of one piece, including the space between the legs as shown in Stage 1. Cut out the other piece only along its outside perimeter. Glue the two pieces together and in turn to the backing for a three-quarter wing spread as shown in Stage 1.

Look at the sketches in Fig. 73. As you can see from the side-view sketch, the head and legs project beyond the stomach. For the face, glue an additional piece of wood 1½″ × 2″ high and for the legs a 2½″ × 2½″ piece. These may be left square, but it will be easier if they are shaped before you glue them in position.

Glue the backing of the eagle to a scrap piece of wood, say 10″ × 17″, with a piece of newspaper between as shown in Stage

Fig. 73a   Eagle, front view

Fig. 73b   Eagle, side view

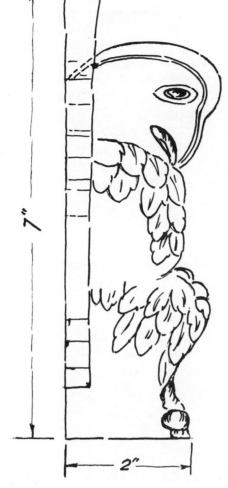

7"

2"

1 and as described previously. When the glue has set, tack the board to your bench or table and you are ready to carve.

Stage 2 shows the rough shape of the eagle boasted with a ½" gouge.

Stage 3 shows the rough gouge marks after they have been smoothed out and the back positioned. Work on the wings as started with the setting-in of the wings.

Stage 4 shows the wings and feathers on the right side set in and positioned. The head has been rough-modeled and the feathers of the body started.

Stage 5 shows the completed carving of the American eagle. (See Fig. 74 for the various stages.)

Fig. 74a   Stage 1

Fig. 74b   Stage 2

Fig. 74c   Stage 3

Fig. 74d   Stage 4

Fig. 74e   Stage 5

83

11 Carving the Zodiac Signs

At this point in your carving, you have already actually executed every cut possible for any piece of sculpture. Although the carving of facial features has not yet been covered, this should present no difficulty. For this practice, there are no better models than the original designs of the zodiac. Sagittarius, Gemini, Virgo, and Aquarius present various positions of the head and face which, when they are executed, will reinforce what you have learned in previous lessons and increase your confidence. In addition, the carving of these particular signs of the zodiac will prepare you properly for any carving situation in which the human head is involved.

The other signs—Aries, Taurus, Cancer, Leo, Libra, Scorpio, and Capricorn—will also be shown in the various stages of carving. It is recommended that they be adapted to your own ideas. Study the illustrations carefully, determine the changes you prefer, and then follow through accordingly.

Remember, the figures are shown to give you practice and experience in using the proper tools to perform the necessary manipulations. Here you have a chance to develop that sweep cut with a deliberate and determined stroke as explained in earlier sections.

The preparation for carving the signs are similar to those given for Pisces in the chapter on laminating woods. The material is pine, basswood, or poplar of one ¾ " × 10" × 10" block for the **bas** or backing and one ¾ " × 8" × 8" block for the raised carvings. In setting up these pieces, follow the procedure given for Pisces.

SAGITTARIUS (November 22-December 21)

Fig. 75 shows the sign of Sagittarius, and Fig. 76, its carving stages. Stage 1 represents the piece as it should appear before carving begins. Note that the shoulders, hair, and arrows are not shown. The shoulders and hair will come below the arrows, which are in the same plane as the backing.

Fig. 75   Sagittarius

Carving
the Zodiac Signs

Fig. 76a   Stage 1

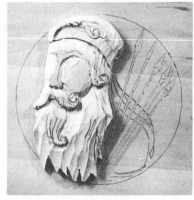

Fig. 76b   Stage 2

Fig. 76c   Stage 3

Fig. 76d   Stage 4

In Stage 2 the prominent lines of the headband, mustache, and outstanding hair and beard are set in and grounded with gouges that best fit the curves.

Next, the nose and eye areas should be rough-shaped with a veining tool and the waste removed. Round the cheeks with a ½″ gouge. The beard shows the rough boasting marks made by a ¾″ gouge. The shoulders and arrows have been sketched in position.

Stage 3 shows the completed carving. Study it carefully. The perimeter of the eye is shaped with a V tool and the eye itself set in with a small curved gouge. The pupil and iris are carved with a small quick gouge.

The circumference is brought out with a ½ " quick gouge and gradually slopes to a ⅜" depth. Before this is done, chase the outline of the arrows with a V tool (small) and gradually remove the waste.

When all the carving is completed, use a medium garnet paper to smooth the face, part of the shoulders, and the arrows. Follow up with #000 garnet paper for a clean, smooth finish.

GEMINI (May 21-June 20)

Figure 77 shows the artist's rendition of the Gemini twins, and Fig. 78, its evolution. In Stage 1, we see how your carving should look when it is prepared. Stage 2 shows the arms, hands, flower, hairline, and chins after they have been set in, grounded, and the waste removed. The cheeks and head hair have been rounded with a ½ " gouge.

In Stage 3 the faces have been rounded and the rough gouge marks removed. The arms and shoulders have been boasted. More boasting has been done on the hair and flowers.

Note the ovular shape of the faces. Keep this in mind when you are carving faces or human heads.

Fig. 77   Gemini

Carving
the Zodiac Signs

Fig. 78a   Stage 1

Fig. 78b   Stage 2

Fig. 78c   Stage 3

Fig. 78d   Stage 4

Fig. 78e   Stage 5

In Stage 4 the eyes, nose, and mouth have been drawn. For this stage you will start on the inside of the nose with a veiner or quick gouge and gradually remove the waste away from the nose toward the outline of the cheeks, forming an egg-shaped curve. The eyes should be brought out with the same veiner and they slant gradually toward the ears in a sort of oval shape.

Note that the chin, forehead, and lips gradually slope toward the extreme outline of the face. Shape the fingers with a small gouge. Boast the hair with a V tool. Shape the lips with small gouges.

The lower lip is shorter than the upper lip. Its fullest part is at the center, where it curves in under the lip slanting toward the chin. Its extreme ends slant toward the ears.

For Stage 5 use a ⅜" flat gouge and smooth out all rough gouge marks.

Complete the circular form with a ½" quick gouge and gradually slope to a ⅜" depth.

To complete the carving, use a medium garnet paper and follow with a #000 fine garnet paper.

VIRGO (August 23-September 22)

Fig. 79 shows the zodiac sign of Virgo and Fig. 80 illustrates the carving steps.

In Stage 1 we see the figure as it should appear before you do any carving.

Fig. 79   Virgo

Carving
the Zodiac Signs

Fig. 80a   Stage 1

Fig. 80b   Stage 2

Fig. 80c   Stage 3

Fig. 80d   Stage 4

For Stage 2 you will set in and ground the face, hairline, neck, and flowers with gouges that best fit the curves; then gradually you should remove all the waste. Note that the flowing hair to the right and left of the figure will be in the same plane as the backing. Actually, if this is removed at the outset, a lot of tedious gouging and waste removal will be eliminated.

In Stage 3 the face has been rounded. Start from the sides of the nose with a veiner or quick gouge and continue up and around into the underside of the eyebrows and remove the waste, slanting gradually to the outline of the face. Use a small quick gouge for the lobes of the nose. Lay out the lips. The top lip is slightly longer than the lower lip and slants to the sides of the face outline. The lower lip slopes toward the cheeks or ear. It is fullest at its center. Use a small veiner or quick gouge under the full part of the lower lip and remove the waste gradually to form the depression under the lower lip.

For Stage 4 clean up all rough areas with a ⅜" or ½" flat gouge and use medium and fine garnet paper on the face, neck, and shoulders.

Study this stage carefully and complete the necessary details as shown in the photo.

AQUARIUS (January 20-February 18)

In Fig. 81 we see the artist's rendition of this zodiac sign. Again, Fig. 82 shows the various stages of the carving. Stage 1 shows the piece as it should appear before you begin.

Fig. 81   Aquarius

Fig. 82a   Stage 1

Fig. 82b   Stage 2

Fig. 82c   Stage 3

Fig. 82d   Stage 4

For Stage 2 you will set in the hair and ear along the forehead and face, the chin and right side of face, and the wrists and hands. Ground the surrounding areas to the depth shown.

Then, with a ¾ " gouge, boast the areas shown with heavy gouge marks.

For Stage 3, with a ½ " flat gouge, remove all the heavy gouge marks and gradually shape the hands, cheeks, and chin with a ⅜ " gouge. Use a ¼ " veiner (fluter) and shape the sides of the nose and underside of the eyebrows. Gradually remove the waste to form the shape of the nose and the upper cheek area. Use the same tool to round off the lobes of the nose and the curved part of the lower part of the cheek.

Shape the lips with a small veiner and bring out the lower lip by using a larger veiner (fluter) on the underside of the lip so that it curves in and down into the chin.

Each time you use the veiner, the projecting sharp ridges must be removed to make a smooth transition with the surrounding area. This is somewhat similar to setting in and removing the waste. Use a ¼ " gouge to shape the hands and a V tool (small) for the water flowing from the vase.

In Stage 4 you should study the completed carving and complete the necessary details as shown. You know what your tools can do. Finally, use a medium garnet paper followed by a fine garnet paper (#000) and go over the face, hands, and shoulders.

ARIES (March 21-April 19)

Fig. 83 is the familiar figure of Aries as the artist has seen it, and Fig. 84, the stages.

Stage 1—not shown—is prepared in a manner similar to that used for the other zodiac representations.

Fig. 83   Aries

Fig. 84a   Stage 2

Fig. 84b   Stage 3

Fig. 84c   Stage 4

For Stage 2 you will set in and ground in around the perimeter of the face with gouges that best fit the curves. Use a ½″ gouge around the horns and in the area of the mane.

In Stage 3 boast the horns with a ½″ shallow gouge. Rough-boast and rough-model around the nose and eye areas with a ¼″ fluter. Use a ¼″ V tool for the mouth and nostrils. Smooth out the rough gouge marks made for the mane and plan the curled-up mane.

For Stage 4 study the completed design and finish your carving accordingly.

In Fig. 85 we see the zodiac symbol for Taurus. Fig. 86 shows the various carving stages.

In Stage 1 you will observe the design as it is prepared for carving.

Fig. 85   Taurus

Fig. 86a   Stage 1

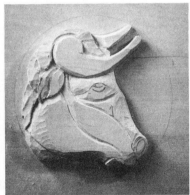

Fig. 86b   Stage 2

Fig. 86c   Stage 3   Fig. 86d   Stage 4

For Stage 2 set in and ground in the horns as shown. The mane should be rough-boasted with a ½ " gouge. You should use a ½ " V tool to set in the muscles of the face.

In the figure illustrating Stage 3 the face has been boasted and the mane carved in a stylized form. The eyes have been set with a small V gouge. The mouth and nose have been shaped somewhat.

Stage 4 shows the facial features after they have been modeled and all the rough gouge marks have been removed. During this stage you will model the eye with the small V gouge and a small gouge. The pupils and the iris are to be set in with a small quick gouge.

The veiner and V tool are used to change the mane. Here the rivulets of the horns are chased with a small veiner.

Study the design and complete the carving with the details shown in the photo.

CANCER (June 21-July 22)

In Fig. 87 is the zodiac sign of Cancer the crab. Fig. 88 illustrates the stages.

Stage 1 shows the sign as it appears before you start to carve.

For Stage 2 you will set in and ground the shell and partly shape the feelers. Then set in, ground, and rough-shape sections of the legs and claws.

Carving
the Zodiac Signs

Fig. 87   Cancer

Fig. 88a   Stage 1

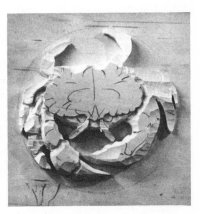

Fig. 88b   Stage 2

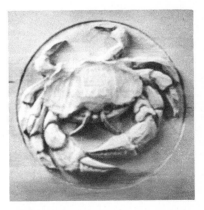

Fig. 88c   Stage 3

Fig. 88d   Stage 4

The figure illustrating Stage 3 shows the shell after it has been boasted with a ½" gouge. The legs and claws are then boasted with a ⅜" gouge.

The V tool is used here for the mouth; then the sides of the claws are rounded.

The feelers should be worked on very carefully with a small gouge.

Figure 96d shows Stage 4, the completed design. Here all rough gouge marks have been removed and the shell and legs have been modeled more finely. The bubbles of the water are set and the background has been brought down to ⅜" depth.

LEO (July 25-August 22)

In Fig. 89 is shown the impressive face of Leo the lion. Again, the following figure—90—shows the various stages you will complete. Stage 1 is the sign as it appears before carving. In Stage 2 you will rough-boast the face.

In Stage 3, set in the features of the face. Use a V tool along the nose and under the eyebrows and mouth.

Fig. 89   Leo

Carving
the Zodiac Signs

Fig. 90a   Stage 1

Fig. 90b   Stage 2

Fig. 90c   Stage 3

Fig. 90d   Stage 4

Set in the eyes with a small V tool. Then use a ⅜″ gouge under the eyebrow over the eyes.

Rough-boast the mane on the right side and then work toward completion of the mane on the left.

Stage 4 shows the completed design. Study it carefully and finish the detailing of the facial features and the mane.

LIBRA (September 23-October 22)

Libra is seen in Fig. 91. Fig. 92 shows the succeeding stages of the carving. Stage 1 illustrates the properly prepared figure.

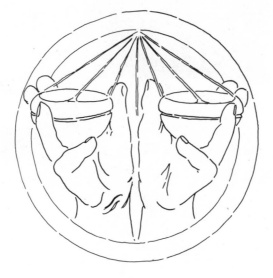

Fig. 91   Libra

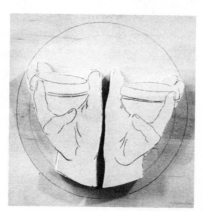

Fig. 92a   Stage 1

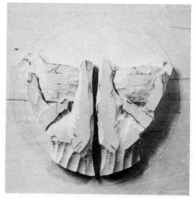

Fig. 92b   Stage 2

100

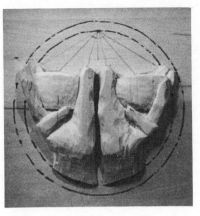

Fig. 92c   Stage 3

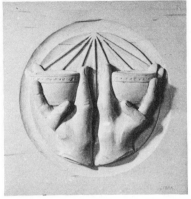

Fig. 92d   Stage 4

In Stage 2 you will carve the fingers holding the cups. Set them in and ground them. Then rough-boast them with a ½ ″ gouge. With the same tool, boast the wrist and palms as shown.

For Stage 3 most of the rough gouge marks should be removed. The fingers are then roughly shaped. Draw the outer and inner circles and position the intersecting lines.

In Stage 4 you should round the outer circumference to meet the inner circle. For this use a ½ ″ quick gouge to a depth of ⅜ ″. With a flat ½ ″ gouge, remove all the gouge marks and shape the fingers with a ⅜ ″ flat gouge. Use a small V tool for the finger-nails and cup borders and chase the intersecting rays with a small V gouge and remove the waste between.

Complete the finishing with medium garnet paper followed with fine grade (#000) of garnet. Do not use sandpaper because the sand may get into the pores of the wood.

SCORPIO (October 23-November 21)

Figure 93 shows Scorpio as this sign looks to the artist. Your preparation of the sign is represented in Fig. 94. Here the legs and claws have been sketched on the surface of the base.

Carving
the Zodiac Signs

Fig. 93 Scorpio

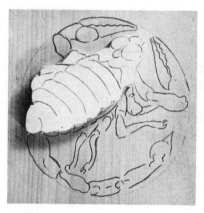

Fig. 94a Stage 1

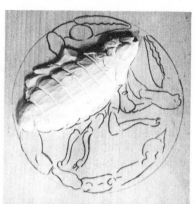

Fig. 94b Stage 2

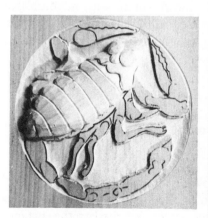

Fig. 94c Stage 3

Fig. 94d Stage 4

In Stage 2 the body has been rough-boasted.

In Stage 3 the legs and claws are shown set in and grounded, with the waste between the various members removed.

By Stage 4 you will have smoothed out all the rough marks of the body and modeled them. The circular ring should be brought to a depth of ⅜" after you use a quick gouge around the circumference. Model the legs and claws, and be sure to keep their upper parts even with or slightly below the surface of the back.

CAPRICORN (December 22-January 19)

Capricorn is illustrated in Fig. 95, and Fig. 96 shows the stages of carving; again, Stage 1 represents the properly prepared piece of wood.

In Stage 2 you will rough-boast the carving. Bring out the face by shaping it with the ½" V tool. Set in the horns with the proper gouges and then do the grounding. Use the ½" gouge to round off the areas shown.

In Stage 3 the mane is shown as a stylized form. Set in the overlapping parts with a V tool, then ground and smooth the piece. If you prefer, this form of mane and whiskers may be left

Fig. 95   Capricorn

Carving
the Zodiac Signs

Fig. 96a   Stage 1

Fig. 96b   Stage 2

Fig. 96c   Stage 3

Fig. 96d   Stage 4

as shown. A careful study of the face will show what kind of tool has been used to form the muscular parts, the eyes, and the eyebrows. The left forehead should be gouged with the concave of the sweep down.

Stage 4 shows the completed Capricorn. The rivulets on the horns are done with a small veiner. In this illustration the mane has been changed with the V tool.

The eye and the pupil and iris have been indented here with a ³⁄₁₆″ quick gouge.

All rough gouge marks should be removed with a ½″ flat gouge.

You can bring out the underside of the eyebrows with a ¼″ veiner (fluter), and cut the inside bottom lid carefully up to the eye to produce a narrow border.

The **zigzag** marks shown along the sides of the cheeks are made with a ¾″ flat gouge. (For further description of the zigzag see "terminology."

Use garnet paper on the face and horns; then study the design and complete the necessary details.

12 Further Examples of Woodcarvings

PIERCED CARVING

You will need a piece of ¾ " mahogany, 21 " × 16 ".

In Fig 97 we see the design as it has been pierced with a scroll saw, then glued to a scrap piece of board with newspaper between.

The triangular border has been gouged down to ½ ". The flowers were brought out by adding ⅜ " wood to the area.

Study the photo and proceed as explained under the section concerned with pierced carving.

106

Further Examples
of Woodcarvings

Fig. 97   Pierced carving for a grill in a ventilating duct

CARVED FRAMES

Each of the frames shown in Fig. 98 is carved from one piece of mahogany ¾ " thick. The measurements for all three styles are listed below.

French design   ¾ " × 14 " × 25 "
Italian design   ¾ " × 20 " × 13½ "
Rococo design   ¾ " × 18½ " × 13½ "

First draw the designs on your wood. Then cut them out with a scroll saw. Next, glue them to boards with newspaper between, and start the carving after the glue has set.

Boast the designs to the required shapes and then model them as shown.

**Further Examples
of Woodcarvings**

Fig. 98a   A French-style
carved frame

Fig. 98b   An Italian-style
carved frame

Fig. 98c   A Rococo-style
carved frame

It is recommended you back up and reinforce these frames with ¼ " plywood. If a frame without a backing should be dropped accidentally, it is likely to break into many pieces.

WALL DECORATIONS

WALL DECORATION 1

To make the first wall decoration in Fig. 99, you will need a piece of poplar 7 " × 25 " overall.

Glue the carved design to the flat base after you have pierced and carved it.

This is an excellent piece to use as a starter for carving wall decorations. It can be used in both the upright and the horizontal positions.

**Further Examples
of Woodcarvings**

Fig. 99a   Wall decoration 1

Fig. 99b   Wall decoration 2

WALL DECORATION 2

Once you have mastered the simpler design, you can try your hand at the second one. This is a pierced carving, made from 6″ × 20″ poplar, mounted on a permanent background of 7″ × 22″ pine.

Your material should be poplar. The wing spread of this carving is 40″; height is 13½″ overall. The body is 3″, including the thickness of the back. The thickest part of the wings measures 2″. These diminish gradually to ¾″ at the tip of the wings. The legs are 2″ thick.

The body has three thicknesses of ¾″ material glued to a ¾″ backing (wings). For the thick part of the wings you should glue extra wood to the area.

To begin, draw the profile of the design on a ¾″ board. Then, following the information given above, prepare the material for the body, head, and legs.

Cut these to the required shape and glue them together. Glue the design with a piece of newspaper on a scrap piece of material. Tack the board on your bench and start carving.

Study the photo in Fig. 100 as you go along and complete the sculpture.

Fig. 100   Alighting American eagle

For this carving you will need poplar—19″ × 13½″ overall. The body at the stomach is 3½″ thick and 4″ from the rear of the backing on which the wings are carved.

While this design is in the half round, very little is needed to make it a full round sculpture.

Draw the profile of the eagle *without* the projecting head and neck on ¾″ poplar material. Draw the eagle, minus the wings, on 1¼″ material with the grain running vertically. Cut out the profiles. On two other pieces of 1¼″ material trace the shape of the eagle from the previously cut-out shape of the eagle. Glue the three similar pieces together and in turn onto the profile of the wings. Align all parts properly, glue, and clamp for three hours.

Glue the back of the eagle (wings) to a scrap piece of lumber, with a piece of newspaper between. When the glue has set, it will be ready to carve.

Tack the board to your bench and rough-boast the entire design. Study Fig. 101 and do your work accordingly. The top

Fig. 101 Standing American eagle

edges of the wings at the body should be a little thicker. For this detail, a ½ ″ or ¾ ″ strip should be glued to these areas before boasting.

BABY OWL

For this carving you will need four pieces of 1½ ″ pine—8½ ″ × 4½ ″ front, 4″ deep.

Trace the profile on each of the four pieces of material. Glue two pieces together for the right section and two pieces for the left section.

Anchor the right side. Boast it to the shape required.

Repeat with the other section. *Make sure it is anchored in the opposite direction.*

When you are satisfied with the boasting, glue the two sections together and complete the boasting in a vise. When all boasting is finished, model the facial features and feathers as shown in Fig. 102.

Fig. 102   Baby owl

CHERUBS

For the cherubs in Fig. 103, you will need poplar, 8½″ × 8½″.

Fig. 103a   Cherub 1

Fig. 103b   Cherub 2

CHERUB 1 (with ribbon on head)

The full head is 5″ high by 4½″, and made up of two ¾″ pieces glued to the wing area, which is ¾″ thick.

Draw the profile of the head on one of the 5″ × 4½″ material and cut it out with a scroll saw. Superimpose the pattern on another 5″ × ½″ piece; trace it and cut it to shape. Glue the cut pieces together and then onto a third piece of wood composing the wing area (8½″ × 8½″ overall).

Note: The hair area to the left is part of the third piece. Sketch the wings, including the hair to the left, and cut this part out with a scroll saw before it is glued to the head pieces.

Now glue the design to a board with newspaper between and start the carving when the glue has set. Study Fig. 103.

CHERUB 2

Follow the same procedure. Study the design and proceed accordingly.

CORNUCOPIA (The Horn of Plenty)

This carving (Fig. 104) is taken from a Hallmark design. Its background is 13″ × 17½″ × ¾″. The applied portion is 15″ × 11″ overall. The material is basswood.

The design, including the leaves, should be drawn on a ¾″ × 15″ × 11″ board, with the grain running horizontally. Use a jigsaw to cut out the shape.

Superimpose the shape on another ¾″ × 15″ × 11″ board and trace it—without the leaves. Glue the pieces together with the first pattern under and then glue to the base or backing of 13″ × 17½″. The base should be a little larger so the design may be tacked to the bench or table. When the carving is completed, the backing can be cut to proper size.

The highest part of the design is the center of the rim of the horn. This part is about 1½″ from the base. The lowest part of the horn is at its end. This is about ⅝″ from the base.

The leaves to the side of the horn vary from ¼″ to ½″ in thickness.

Further Examples
of Woodcarvings

Fig. 104 Cornucopia
Woodcarving taken from Hall-
mark design. © Hallmark Cards,
Inc. Used by permission.

The green pepper at the center of the design should be left at
the height of the rim of the horn.

Arrange the remainder of the fruits and vegetables at varying
heights.

Study the design and determine the proper tools to use for
each of the fruits and vegetables.

In starting the carving, boast the entire design and set in the
various items before you attempt to do any modeling.

SCHOOL EMBLEM
(Samuel Gompers Vocational High School)

Your material for this should be mahogany. Overall, its measurements are 12″ × 12″.

The center insignia depicts the various trades taught at the school—the gear for the automotive trade, the lighting flash for the electrical trade, and the caliper for the architecture and mechanical drafting courses. The laurel leaf was used by the Greeks to crown visitors in games and later as a distinction in learning.

The wings at the top of the design signify achievement.

The backing panel for this carving (Fig. 105) is ½″ veneer upon which the precut laurel leaves and wings are glued. The modeling is done directly on the panel.

By using variations of the carving you have learned, you can make your own school (or club) emblem.

Fig. 105   School emblem

CADUCEUS
(Physician's Symbol)

To make the caduceus in Fig. 106, you will need 10″ × 14½″ pine.

The top part of the wings is ¾″, diminishing to ¼″ at the bottom.

The snakes taper down at the sides from ½″ at the mouths of the snakes to ¼″ at the tail ends.

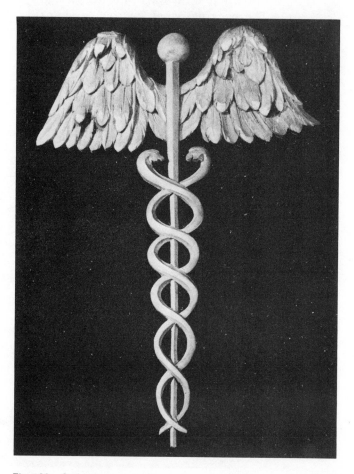

Fig. 106 Caduceus

MUSIC STAND

To make the music stand in Fig. 107, which has been designed for a grand piano, you will need 12″ × 25″ poplar on a walnut base.

This carving is made from one piece of wood. The volutes of the scrolls and the flowers were made to rise above the main carving by gluing additional wood to those areas.

Fig. 107   Music stand

119

Fig. 108, from the collection of Mr. and Mrs. C. Vitanza, is an excellent example of appliqué work, where wood is glued to wood to bring out portions of the carving in higher relief. Use 7″ × 9″ walnut to make this project.

Fig. 108   Clock case

The yearling in Fig. 109 is carved from a solid block of wood, 6″ × 8″ poplar, on a pine base.

Fig. 109   Yearling

The head of Christ in Fig. 110 is made of 6″ × 9″ walnut, mounted on a pine background (for the cross) whose dimensions are 10″ × 12″.

Fig. 110   Christ head

WALL BRACKET

Use 7″ × 9″ poplar to make the wall bracket shown in Fig. 111, which is carved from a solid block of wood.

Fig. 111   Wall bracket

13 Finishing Your Carvings

A well-done carving, with its clean cuts and the shine of wood produced by sharp chisels, doesn't need any "finishing" other than some protective coat to keep it clean and preserve the wood. This, of course, refers to work of art or individual pieces which in themselves are a complete entity. Carvings applied to furniture or a part of a decorative scheme or design are finished to blend in with the surrounding surfaces.

In any event, if the carver feels that something other than a protective coat is needed he should experiment with a desired finish on scrap wood before applying it to the finished carving.

The finishes given below are suitable for individual carvings as well as for carvings applied to a decorative design.

NATURAL FINISH

Remove any pencil marks with a scraper or cleaning eraser, and any soiled spots with a detergent or soap and water. When the piece is thoroughly dry, apply a thin coat (wash coat) of shellac, made by reducing the shellac 4 to 1 with alcohol. When this is dry, go over the work with fine steel wool, then apply a coat of paste floor wax with a cloth or a brush. After 15 minutes rub it briskly with a soft cloth or shoebrush. Repeat the waxing procedure after 2 hours for a finer finish.

FLAT FINISH

To produce a hand-rubbed effect without the labor involved, apply a flat varnish or lacquer directly to the base wood. If a finer finish is desired, the flat varnish can be rubbed when dry with fine steel wool lubricated with paste wax.

STAIN WAX

Penetrating oil stains are available in many colors. They are easy to apply and will not raise the grain of the wood. Since the stains will penetrate more deeply in the end graining or soft spots of the wood, these areas should be wiped immediately after the stain is applied.

Manufacturer's directions should always be followed for best results. Normally, the stain is brushed on evenly and allowed to penetrate. The surplus is then wiped off with a rag. Start wiping with light strokes and increase or decrease the pressure according to the shade desired. After 24 hours another coat of stain may be applied if necessary. When the piece is dry (24 hours), apply a wash coat of shellac (4-1) and follow this with the waxing procedure given above for a natural finish.

ANTIQUING

You can shade a finished work by applying an oil pigment worked with raw linseed oil. In many cases a raw umber oil pig-

125

ment mixed with linseed oil will give an aged appearance. Apply the material to the work and wipe the excess off to expose the highlights. With a little practice on scrap wood of the same material as the carving, you will soon know whether to add more linseed oil to make the stain lighter or to add more pigment to make it darker.

Antiquing (glazing, pickling, highlighting, etc.) can be done with virtually any color of oil pigment to produce a desired result in color.

Things to Remember in Carving

Anchoring.　Never cut unless the piece of wood is firmly anchored. Become familiar with the clamping-down methods.

Bent riffler.　Use in tough-to-get-at spots.

Carpenter's chisel.　Use firmer for set-ins. If carpenter's chisel is used, set the flat side against the design.

Carving facial features.　If you are not sure of the gouge cuts for these items, practice on a scrap piece before cutting into the actual carving. Always start from the sides of the nose with the veining tool. Use V tool for eyes. Round off eye part after setting in to shape.

Carving leaves.　Involve all possible curves. If these are mastered, any other carving will be easy. Remember that leaves need not be made to look real; establish the characteristic shape, then simplify by keeping to the general twisting action. Also remember that delicate leaves have a tendency to break

127

off at the edges of the points; watch the grain, and, in most cases, start the cut from the points.

Cuts. Make them deliberately and remove waste without wriggling (twist and turning). Do not rock the gouge to remove waste.

Diagonal cutting. This is safer than cutting with the grain.

Emery powder. Use on strop.

Gouge cuts. Remove with a flat gouge.

Grain. Always consider the grain. A smooth cut will be influenced by the behavior of the wood.

Relief carving. Watch the grain! It may be quite easy to cut down into wood in some sections, but quite different in other parts.

Rounding. In this process, gouge a little at a time.

Smoothing out. Obtain the general form first (boast) then smooth out gouge marks with a flat gouge.

Sweep cut. The wavy and twisting forms of leaves are best modeled by the sweep cut. Two fingers are on the blade, with thumb under as in Fig. 18. Start the cut with your right hand pushing the gouge and with one sweep of the tool perform three movements with one stroke. Move the gouge down, around, and up and down as the leaf on curve undulates. The left hand guides the tool to either side as required and at the same time the tool is raised or lowered by a wrist action to conform to the wavelike form of the curve.

Undercutting. Use the V tool at a 45° angle (see Fig. 112).

Fig. 112

Veining leaves. Use a V tool.

Working on a carving. Work on the entire panel—don't concentrate on one point.

Working with two hands. Try to learn to work the tool with either hand. Keep the hand that is not guiding the tool in back of the cutting edge.

Zigzagging. Hold the tool straight down and "walk" it by swaying it from side to side in a zigzag fashion.

Sources
of Material

Albert Constantine & Son, Inc.
2050 Eastchester Road, Bronx, New York 10461
   Chisels, gouges; carving woods; all carving materials

Craftsman Wood Service
2729 South Mary Street, Chicago, Illinois 60608
   Carving woods; tools

Sculpture House
38 East 30th Street, New York, New York 10016
   All carving tools and accessories

Frank Mittermeir
3577 East Tremont Avenue, Bronx, New York 10465
   All carving tools and accessories

Bibliography

ALLER, DORIS, *Sunset Wood Carving Book*. New York: Dover, 1962.

BRIDGMAN, GEORGE B., *Constructive Anatomy*. New York. Dover, 1973.

DURST, ALAN, *Woodcarving,* rev. ed. New York: Viking, 1969.

LACEY, JOHN L., *How to Do Woodcarving*. New York: Arco Publishing Co., 1975.

LELAND, CHARLES C., *Wood Carving*. New York: Pitman & Sons, 1931.

MUGNAMI, JOSEPH, and JANICE LOVOOS, *Drawing, A Search for Form*. New York: Reinhold, 1965.

ROOD, JOHN, *Sculpture in Wood*. New York: Oxford University Press, 1968.

SKINNER, FREDA, *Wood Carving*. New York: Bonanza Books, 1961.

131

SLOBODKIN, LOUIS, *Sculpture: Principles and Practice.* New York: Dover, 1973.

TANGERMAN, E. J., *Whittling and Woodcarving.* New York: Dover, 1962.

WALKER, ERNEST P., et al., *Mammals of the World.* Baltimore: The Johns Hopkins Press, 1964.

WILLIAMS, J. H., *Elephant Bill.* New York: Doubleday & Co., 1950.

Index

133